Materials Management

An Executive's Supply Chain Guide

Stan C. McDonald

WILEY

John Wiley & Sons, Inc.

Published by John Wiley & Sons, Inc., Hoboken, New Jersey.

Published simultaneously in Canada.

For general information on our other products and services, or technical support, please contact our Customer Care Department within the United States at 800-762-2974, outside the United States at 317-572-3993 or fax 317-572-4002.

Wiley also publishes its books in a variety of electronic formats. Some content that appears in print may not be available in electronic books.

For more information about Wiley products, visit our Web site at http://www.wiley.com.

Library of Congress Cataloging-in-Publication Data:
McDonald, Stan, 1952-
    Materials management : an executive's supply chain guide / Stan McDonald.
        p. cm.
    Includes bibliographical references and index.
    ISBN 978-0-470-43757-5 (cloth)
    1. Business logistics–Management.   2. Material requirements planning.
3. Inventory control.   I. Title.
    HD38.5.M396 2009
    658.5—dc22   2008040317

100627708X

Printed in the United States of America
10 9 8 7 6 5 4 3 2 1

This book is dedicated to several senior managers who had faith in me to resolve some of the challenges in materials management:

Tomas Hagberg, who inspired me to move up in my first organization.

Mike Sanna, who is a superior manager and whose support for my materials efforts is sincerely appreciated.

Jim McManus, who had faith in me to resolve some difficult issues in a Mexican plant. My family will remember your kindness.

Ron Pratt, who gave me the opportunity to achieve my lifelong dream of director with the independence to make the decisions that were best for materials operations.

My wife, whose undying support has made it possible to work for months at a time away from home.

CONTENTS

PREFACE

This book was written to provide an overview of the most critical parts of the materials management process and provide the *proven answer* to any inventory management problem. The proven answer to an inventory management problem is the closed-loop system of controls described. None of the parts described in the book should be compromised. A failure to implement any part of this process will result in a compromise of the inventory integrity, and the system will eventually break down. Inventory integrity is the driver of a good materials management system. A good materials system provides an unbroken supply of components to production.

As a prerequisite to implementing the system described in the book, there needs to be a complete focus on bill of materials accuracy and a resolution to any scrap reporting process that is lacking controls.

This book describes methods to ensure bill of materials accuracy. If your company has bill of materials accuracy issues, it must incur the expense of correcting them by focusing resources on reviewing all of the bills of materials.

There is no well-defined method to control scrap reporting. Accurate scrap reporting relies completely on the attitudes of the workers in the plant. This book notes some inherent issues with reporting scrap accurately. In addition, it also describes some methods that are better than others.

Companies need to look at the scrap percentage reported combined with the loss of inventory to obtain a more accurate scrap rate. It could be argued that inventory write-down is not entirely caused by unreported scrap but other mismanagement in the system. The other mismanaged issues are those that can be corrected—notably, issues with cycle counting adjustments, bill of materials issues, or any other controllable issue. If these issues are corrected, then there is no other reason for an inventory write-down except for not reporting scrap correctly.

Once a true scrap rate is determined, the total costs per annum should be compared in order to correct scrap contributors. Major scrap contributors are usually poor quality, equipment failures, and processes that have not been perfected.

As an executive manager, your only contact with materials control people in the plant may be with reviewing month-end reports. Inventory numbers that do not meet the company goals and/or out-of-control freight costs may be prevalent. Sometimes they are overlooked or ignored. Any excuse for poor materials performance is unacceptable; reasons need to be fully disclosed with corrective actions provided.

This book explains some of the inner workings of the materials process and describes the best operating system guaranteed to eliminate issues surrounding ineffective materials management.

Materials management is not a profession like medicine or law where a specialized degree and passing a board or bar examination is required. There are no common rules and guidelines that all companies can follow because processes are different. A company's proficiency in materials management, however, is directly related to the degree of responsibility, authority, and visibility in the organization.

The focus for the last decade has been primarily on optimizing manufacturing. Most corporations have succeeded in reducing waste, elevating plant output to the highest levels.

With so much focus on manufacturing, there has been little or no attention to the issues in materials management. The supply of components for the manufacturing process, high inventories, high freight

costs, or poor customer delivery may be affecting company performance, and these issues need to be addressed.

Some companies that have recognized the need to focus on inventory
reduction and freight management have attempted to implement better
control practices. The champions of this effort are not manufacturing
companies; rather they are the third-party logistics companies that have
been formed to manage the inventory for companies.

More and more companies are looking to use as much plant floor
space for manufacturing as possible, and the desire to attain just-in-time
deliveries of materials has pushed the inventory control from plants to
third-party logistics companies that understand how to meter parts into
the plant.

The automotive industry is pushing the control of inventory into
third-party logistics management for a number of reasons. Automotive
companies have found that they can force suppliers to own the materials up to the point of shipment from the third-party sequencer. Payment
is often delayed until a vehicle rolls off the assembly line. The benefit of
not having to manage storage of components in an original equipment
manufacturer (OEM) site is a major cost savings, freeing up cash for the
OEM.

Through the years I have kept up with the most state-of-the-art systems for inventory control first by studying Ford's systems and now by
studying the best-in-class third-party logistics companies. Such companies compete on their ability to manage inventory and then sequence
that inventory to their customers. Because their whole business is predi-
cated on inventory management, they have to have the best systems of
control. If you want to see the best-in-class systems, visit several top
third-party logistics companies that employ the scanning process as the
main controller of inventory accuracy.

The key to third-party logistics companies' success is their ability to
implement the best scanning systems available. The best in class employ
radio-frequency (RF) scanning systems. The best third-party control
systems simply adopt this practice: "If you see it and you can move it,
then you can scan it and then you can find it later."

Every single movement of material is controlled by scanning in the best third-party logistics companies. This allows for the maximization of space, and space equates to cash. Product is always placed in the first available location, not by allocated locations. First in, first out (FIFO, a method of using inventory) is controlled by scanning. When a component is required, the scanner shows where the oldest inventory is located.

The best materials practices available are not without cost. The correct software and the appropriate scanning tools are essential to the success of this process. The implementation of the best practices will prove to reduce costs that would otherwise be incurred with poor inventory control.

In this book, you will not find many buzzwords to describe methods because the selection of words is immaterial to incorporating the best systems. Some companies expound on using words that describe what they are trying to achieve as an organization. Many of these words are used for a short time, replaced by a new set or words, and then discarded again. Words alone do not make a plant excel, and many companies adopt buzzwords that mean nothing to improving actual operations. Using "marketplace" as the description of an inventory storage site does not make for better inventory management if nothing has changed except the words we use. The corrective actions that are taken to improve inventory management are conducive to the best materials management.

To prove the point about buzzworks, we can go back in time when the best management practice was "world-class operations." The concept of world-class operations lasted a few years and was dropped after its founder, Tom Peters, faded from the limelight because the processes he depicted really did not contribute to improving the bottom line.

ACKNOWLEDGMENTS

Thanks to the Ford Motor Company logistics department for the valuable knowledge learned from its Web-based inventory-tracking systems.

Thanks to Toyota for an in-depth understanding of its inventory control Kaban (card control) system.

Thanks to Nissan Motors for their receiving and warehousing management systems.

Thanks to Ryder logistics for an opportunity to review their third-party supply chain logistics systems.

Thanks to TNT Logistics for a detailed review of their supply chain logistics and warehouse management systems.

Thanks to Panalpina Logistics for the knowledge gained of overseas logistics operations.

This book contains some of the philosophies of President Abraham Lincoln while he was in office.

Thanks to President Ronald Reagan for his unique ability to create some of the most famous lines and quips in U.S. history that are revered for their brevity and conciseness.

Thanks to Lee Iaccoca for sharing some of his management ideals that launched Chrysler from bankruptcy to profitability.

CHAPTER I

BEFORE COMPUTER SYSTEMS

INVENTORY CARD CONTROL SYSTEM

Before computer systems were available to companies to use for materials planning, the manual systems in use contained key elements of today's current software-driven systems. Before the age of computer-generated inventory control systems, many companies used a card management system that contained columns for logging inventory information. The system, although simplistic, served the purpose: managing inventory.

The best control system used preprinted cards for logging daily inventory transactions. The cards generally fit into a tub file that accommodated at least 250 cards with metal separators for each row of 25 cards. Half-circle cutouts on the bottom of the control cards fit snugly into round vertical holding rods on the bottom of the tub, similar to some index file cardholders.

To conserve space in the tube file, the inventory control cards were placed on top of each other with only the part number showing in consecutive part number order. The part number was written or stamped on each inventory control card, and each card was cut on a 45-degree angle to make pulling cards out of the file easier.

Like today's modern-day computer systems, control cards contained all the information required for the particular component. The card system provided columns for the date, the on-order quantity, received quantity in inspection, the amount issued to manufacturing, and the running balance on hand. Spaces were available on the top of the card to record the part number description, the minimum, the maximum, the reorder point, the lead time, the forecast, and the actual usage. Most card systems also provided areas for the usage by product.

The card system was managed entirely by posting all activities manually in pencil for every transaction. Pencil entries were preferred for ease of erasure.

With this system, copies of all transactions that required posting had to be available for the planner. The paperwork involved was high volume, considering the number of purchase orders, the receiving paperwork, and the pick tickets generated on a daily basis.

The process of reordering materials involved filling out a two-part form with all the pertinent information and then sending a copy to a buyer. The planner then had to match the paperwork with the completed paperwork from the buyer to ensure that the release was issued to the supplier. The release number and date of delivery was then posted to the control card.

The drawbacks to the system included posting errors, addition and subtraction errors, lost paperwork, and errors on the data received. In spite of these types of errors, the system provided a good management tool in those precomputer days.

Although using this manual system was time consuming, it did have an advantage over modern software systems: All of the information was kept in one place. The card system contained all of the information about a particular part number on one document. Computer systems contain all of the information that the card system contained and more; however, to access that information, multiple screens must be used or a report must be generated from the system.

ADVANTAGES OF THE MANUAL CARD SYSTEM
OF INVENTORY CONTROL

Controlling inventory using a manual system provided another advantage that computer systems do not have. Since the manual system requires the constant posting of data, the planner was more in tune with the parts that were being controlled. With the advent of computerized inventory control, planners became more distant from the actual components being controlled. In many cases, planners are not aware of part numbers and inventory balances.

Using the computer system has removed some planners from the visual interfacing that took place before material requirements planning (MRP). Sometimes such separation from the components managed becomes a disadvantage, as when there is a crisis with a component shortage. If substitutes are available, the substitution is bypassed because the planner cannot recognize that another part is similar to the one that is required because the MRP numbering scheme is usually assigned in numerical order.

Before computer systems, many organizations used part number schemes that allowed users to identify components in classes of parts. Planners could relate to components so that they could make substitution decisions by comparing similar part numbers that would be associated with the same product that could be reworked as a substitution. With the advent of computer systems, many companies decided that the part number scheme was immaterial. The debate around restoring the part number schemes continues to this day, but the advantage to using such schemes is obvious, especially when planners do not visually manage materials.

The usage of a part by product line was always clearly written on the control card; in today's control systems, the inventory management system is located on a separate screen from the inventory on-hand screen. With the card system, planners were more aware of the use of a particular part by product line and therefore more familiar with the product structure. This allowed planners to recognize potential part use issues.

For example, if there were three screws used for a product A and three screws used for product B, but product B was larger, the planner might question the usage for product B. A good planner would recognize a problem when calculating the minimum and maximum levels using the usage numbers and the forecast.

Modern computer systems bury the usage in multiple setup screens that planners need to consciously access. The computer system does not give planners the immediate visual opportunity to compare the use of a component across several different assemblies.

Computer systems automatically update minimum and maximum inventory level, which prevents planners from associating use to product lines. Most of the time, errors in bills of materials leading to usage errors are not detected until there is a shortage of material or a buildup in inventory because the usage for a part is incorrect.

BILL OF MATERIALS ACCURACY

The importance of entering bills of materials into the computer system accurately is not debatable; however, too many companies experience less-than-satisfactory bills of materials accuracy. This is why it is so important to verify all data entered into the system supporting the bills of materials.

Many companies rely on the corporate engineering department to enter the bills of materials correctly into the system. Without a visual verification of materials used in the actual production process, chances are high that there will be some mistakes. The materials department inherits these mistakes in the form of shortages or excessive inventory.

PICK TICKET SYSTEM

Before the computer system of inventory control, planners relied on pick tickets, which were generally completed by the warehouse personnel who moved the containers to the production line. As with any manual system, errors in calculating the total amounts taken and thus written on the pick ticket were fairly common. The overstatement of inventory caused by the understatement of parts withdrawn for the assembly line meant an eventual stock shortage. The computer system of inventory control has eliminated use of pick tickets to reduce inventory balances; the computer system reduces part number inventory balances automatically as finished goods are entered into the system.

ADVANTAGE OF COMPUTER-GENERATED INVENTORY CONTROL SYSTEMS

The overall advantage of computer systems is the automation and elimination of the manual postings and most of the paperwork. Computer systems are not free from errors, since the bills of materials and the reporting of finished goods have to be 100 percent in order to achieve inventory accuracy perfection.

Computer systems have created a new set of inventory accuracy issues caused by incorrect manual and scanned entries. Unless the human element is eliminated, changing from manual entries to a simple scanning system will not correct entry errors. The saying "garbage in, garbage out" is well known in regard to inventory inaccuracies with computer-managed inventory.

The basic computer-controlled inventory system eliminates the calculations that planners performed, but it does not eliminate the errors. With card-controlled inventory systems, planners had to calculate the use for every part number using forecasted numbers. They had to calculate the minimum and maximum levels in order to release materials from the supply base. The computer system is not capable of correcting inaccurate minimum inventory and maximum inventory levels generated by MRP when there is a usage error. This is because the MRP system does not display the usage on the same screen as where the minium and maximum are located.

What is the advantage of computer-generated inventory control systems versus manual systems? The real advantage of computer systems is the speed of information and the ability to collect real-time information in various formats.

There has been no real improvement in inventory accuracy with the shift from the manual card-controlled system to the computer-controlled system primarily because we continue to use manual input and output without controls and methods that ensure accuracy.

Some people believed that if manual scanning systems were added to inventory management, all of the inaccuracy issues would be solved. This is not true; a simple scanning process is manually driven and therefore error prone.

Adding a manual scanning process for receiving in components speeds up the process of data entry but does not guarantee correctness. No one can guarantee that 100 percent of all items received will be scanned correctly.

Nor does adding a manual scanning process for finished goods guarantee inventory accuracy. There is always someone who forgets to scan a box or someone who takes out finished goods boxes for quality review and reports the product into the system again.

A simple manual scanning process alone does not prevent the shipping of extra materials in error to the customer. There is always a chance that someone will leave a box off the truck or ship an additional box in error.

This book reveals how to use computer systems, scanning, and some other methods to gain 100 percent inventory accuracy.

CHAPTER 2

MATERIAL REQUIREMENTS PLANNING

FOUNDATION FOR MATERIAL REQUIREMENTS PLANNING

Material requirements planning (MRP) is a system that was designed to compute the material needs of the plant, internally and externally. It is not very different from one software system to another. The materials principles in all MRP software systems enable anyone to manage any brand of computer system that a company is using for materials management. The differences in the systems are the location of the planning, shipping, and release control information. Some software packages are more complex than others are because they contain more features supposedly designed to improve inventory control.

Some software packages are better than others because they have features that make the system quicker and easier to input and extract information. Any software package is only as good as the level of accuracy in the system.

MRP is neither the problem nor the root cause for inefficiencies in the material procurement process. The notion that MRP does not work is a fallacy. MRP is a super calculator that provides output data based on selected criteria that are placed into the system. Since MRP is a perfect system, it depends on perfect information in order to provide perfect results. MRP may not work for many companies because of incorrect input/output into the system.

MRP is the process of generating *planned* and *firmed* releases to suppliers, internally and externally. MRP reads the customer orders, forecasts, and the master schedule, or a combination thereof, and then processes the information through the bills of materials in order to generate the demand for the components and raw materials. MRP will calculate new planned releases every time it is generated, changing the delivery date and quantity based on the latest information in the system.

Once a release is changed to firm by the computer system or a planner MRP does not move the date or change the quantity. In order to increase or decrease the quantity or change the delivery date, the user must manually change the firm orders.

MRP will not place a new supplier release before the date of the first firmed planned order; therefore, all components placed with firm orders must be reviewed for MRP-generated action messages every time MRP is generated. Action messages are a part of the MRP system that are designed to give a planner suggestions to move the dates of orders forward or reverse in time. If a planner fails to review the message to increase a firm order, there may be a shortage in the near future.

In the early days of MRP, most companies generated new requirements once per week. This operation, generally performed at night, was referred to as the "nightly job stream." Today computers have much greater efficiency and memory, so MRP can be generated on a daily basis. When MRP is generated daily, the releases are sent to suppliers daily. If releases change dramatically from one MRP to another, suppliers are going to complain and distrust the new shipping releases. As discussed, such problems mean that planning and inventory accuracy issues need to be resolved because there is no stability in the system.

When there is no stability in a system that shows minimal or no immediate changes to the supplier orders, releases should be sent to suppliers less frequently. In general, the materials management system should generate releases daily. In Chapter 20, a best practice addresses the issue of varying releases.

The American Production and Inventory Control Society (APICS), an organization dedicated to the training and education of people in the materials field, started out with a small membership and rapidly gained popularity in the 1970s through the 1980s. With the advent of so many changes in the manufacturing world, the leadership of APICS continued to evolve in the 1990s, changing its area of expertise to include operations management. Today's APICS is dedicated to educating people in a wide variety of businesses, and the organization has evolved into providing insight into operations management.

In the past, many major corporations required materials management employees to have APICS certification. Today, although many companies still prefer to hire people with APICS certification, it is no longer a common requirement.

The certification process from APICS covers a variety of subjects, which a person must understand fully in order to pass a few very comprehensive tests. Upon passing all of the testing requirements, a person receives a written certification from APICS. Such APICS certification helps people understand materials principles but does not teach best practices. An APICS-certified person is not likely to outclass someone who has practical experience.

Oliver Wright, the developer of MRP, thought that he had discovered the perfect process to eliminate shortage and control issues with inventory management. What he did not realize was that the system was not error proof and that it was totally dependent on perfect information. Like other systems, any MRP system becomes practically worthless when lack of inventory accuracy causes supply and production issues.

A computer system is logical and depends on perfect information to provide the required results. If a company could provide its MRP system with perfect information, there would be no need to attempt to develop systems to augment inventory control. Since it is highly improbable that any company has attained perfection in data entered and retrieved from its MRP system, systems for controlling materials must be developed that have a higher level of accuracy. These methods are described in Chapter 20.

IMPORTANCE OF PLANNING PARAMETERS

The poor output of an MRP system is the product of two basic groups of information: parameters and data input/output. The term "parameters" here refers to all of the selections, options, and data required that is controlled by populating fields in MRP to generate order release and shipping information correctly. The phrase "data input/output" refers to all of the information fed into the system, either electronically or manually.

Since a vast number of planning parameters is required to control an enormous amount of information correctly, the odds that everything will work perfectly all of the time are near zero. Incorrect planning parameters in the system are directly related to component shortages, causing lost manufacturing time and possibly premium freight expenditures.

Some of the most important planning parameters are discussed in the next few paragraphs below. Planning parameters that control lead time from the supply base must be accurate in order to generate accurate releasing information to the suppliers. There are two types of lead times in regard to the supply base: manufacturing time and expected delivery time.

The first lead time is the manufacturing time it takes the supplier to make a new component from start to finish. When a company is launching a new product, manufacturing lead time is considered the initial time it takes the supplier to procure raw materials, build, and then ship to the customers' dock.

The second type of lead time is the expected delivery time in days or hours from the supplier on a continued basis. Customers in today's marketplace expect supplier lead times to be equal to the ship time, plus some safety days. Suppliers are expected to maintain a level of stock on hand that enables customers to order on demand.

In order for suppliers to accommodate customers with shorter lead times, suppliers need to rely on customer forecasts that cover the entire time it takes the supplier to procure raw materials and to produce the parts. Because the lead time to customers is the ship time, customers must exercise extreme care when maintaining the lead-time parameter. Many MRP systems distinguish between the lead times by providing a place to enter both supplier manufacturing lead time and transit time. It is advisable not to use both of these lead times, since the system adds them together.

Another critical planning parameter is the make-or-buy parameter. If a component is incorrectly labeled as a "make" part, MRP will not generate a release to the supplier for purchase. If this error is not caught in time, the net result is generally a part shortage in the plant.

Still another critical planning parameter governs the amount of product to be ordered from the suppliers. Some suppliers ship in standard packages, which are actually a good idea and a requirement for any bar code scanning system. The planning parameter must be set so that releases are issued in multiples of standard packs from the supplier. Generally, code letters or numbers are entered into the parameter field to govern the release line-item amount from a supplier.

Small parts that are very inexpensive are sometimes coded for several months of supply. When a release is sent to a supplier, the amount required is added for a period and then ordered as one line item. This enables a plant to order some hardware in bulk instead of a standard pack at a time.

UNDERSTANDING THE IMPACT OF MRP

Most operations managers focus on one issue when it comes to materials control—*part shortages*—even when the assembly line managers knowingly or unknowingly contribute to the problem. Part shortages are the leading cause of downtime in many facilities. Depending on the severity of the problem, the action taken to attempt to resolve it will vary from one extreme to another.

Because of the lack of understanding of how to manage the complexity of the MRP system, materials and operations people are generally at odds. Materials people are inclined to say that the lack of scrap reporting is the primary culprit of inventory accuracy, while manufacturing people are inclined to say that materials people just have no idea how to release parts correctly on time for delivery. There is some truth to both statements, especially when fires are raging in the plant with numerous expedited shipments and extensive downtime caused by part shortages.

In many cases, the lack of components in a facility can cloud some of the issues that are additional causes of downtime. Digging out from firefighting can be a complicated process; however, with correct methods, firefighting can be stopped.

Although some may claim that that data input of 95 percent accuracy is acceptable, that level of accuracy should never be regarded as acceptable with an MRP system. The MRP system relies on 100 percent accuracy, and any percentage below that will cause issues at some point. Since there is no known method of attaining 100 percent MRP accuracy, plants must settle for the highest level attainable by implementing sound procedures and guidelines to control the input/ output and planning parameters. The fact that obtaining 100 percent accuracy is improbable will always result in some part shortages and expediting.

Correcting inventory accuracy is the first step toward resolving the control problem. This book presents another alternative to ordering materials in conjunction with MRP, which has proven to be much more successful than relying on MRP alone to generate requirements.

The best place to start increasing the accuracy of data from the MRP system is by controlling parameters in the system. All planning fields must be correct in order for the proper calculations to occur. Incorrect, misuse, or lack of proper planning parameters will create issues with the proper generation of MRP. Perceptive materials people generate lists of planning parameters by part number and then review those lists for accuracy. If materials control ensures that the planning parameters are

EXHIBIT **2.1**   *Level of Material Control in Your Company*

Questions:	No = 0 Yes = 1

1. Are there daily parts shortages of materials in the plant?
2. Are parts shortages affecting the production output?
3. Does the physical inventory shrink exceed 1 percent?
4. Is premium freight excessive?
5. Is normal freight excessive?
6. Are monthly adjustments for cycle counts excessive?
7. Does the company have expediters or similar people? .
8. Is the downtime caused primarily by part shortages?
9. Does the inventory exceed seven days?

Total:

correct, the materials people can concentrate on other issues that are keeping MRP from being accurate.

Exhibit 2.1 lists nine questions that will reveal the severity of the control issues in the plant. The total of all the answered questions will show the degree of the problem. The closer to 0, the better the management system is. Even a score of 1 implies that there are times when the plant lacks components to keep manufacturing from experiencing downtime. Generally, a lack of a component equates to an expense that the plant must absorb in the form of premium freight or the cost of lost time and labor absorption.

Any amount other than zero reflects a less-than-perfect system. In order to develop adequate material management systems, most companies need to address the nine questions in the exhibit.

Any plant that relies solely on MRP for the generation of releases to suppliers, manufacturing, and customers is likely to have a high number.

CHAPTER 3

THE RAGING FIRE AND FIREFIGHTING

BURNING UP COMPANY PROFITS

The "raging fire" is synonymous with inventory control practices that fail to provide a smooth and consistent flow of materials into a company; thus the process is out of control. A general lack of understanding of planning concepts at all levels of the company is what ignites the fire. This lack of both understanding and the methods to correct the situation perpetuate inventory inaccuracy. Once inventory accuracy is compromised, the whole materials system is doomed.

At some point in the company's history, a semblance of inventory management may have existed. However, through its ineffectiveness, changes occurred that started a raging fire of expediting and out-of-control system planning.

Some plants lose control when a new process is introduced into manufacturing, when new product lines are introduced with poor communication with materials management, or when the bulk of the materials staff resigns or is replaced. If a plant makes a bad decision and hires a materials manager without the expertise to manage the process, good practices often wither away, which directly affects delivery from the supply base and to customers.

Because of cost constraints, many companies have eliminated the corporate function in materials management that is capable of ensuring that new product lines and engineering changes are launched properly. This corporate department is commonly known as "advance planning." Chapter 21 explains the advantages of this department.

If a company is constantly changing engineering levels, adding new product lines, or making major product line adjustments, it should have a materials team designated to manage changes. With a good materials team in place, the plant materials group can continue to focus on plant issues while the materials team focuses on getting the supply base up to speed on new products. Most corporate materials groups that focus on change management are also responsible for ensuring the new launches are timely. Timely launches equate directly to successful launches.

Management that is unable to provide the support to the materials effort often starts fires. Solving the problems requires experienced materials people who have managed systems effectively. Staffing an inventory department with inexperienced personnel and the thinking that "anyone can do it" will result in the start or continuation of a raging fire.

Materials control is complex. Success requires a good understanding of how to use and maintain the system parameters and manage the perpetual inventory accuracy. The executive should compare the contribution of costs of an inept materials department to the bottom-line profits with premium freight, excess freight, stock shortages, and poor customer delivery. If the total dollars lost from materials mismanagement is excessive, the executive should look at cost avoidance by hiring better-caliber personnel in materials management. Too many plants overlook the importance of hiring a professional materials manager when needed; instead, they take people from the plant and expect them to understand how to manage a complex system.

The many inaccuracies imposed on the materials department usually begin with inaccurate bills of materials. Inaccurate bills of materials generally are caused by the company's lack of follow-up or finalization systems. Even when a bill of materials is correct at inception, the changes made in the plant or from the engineering department may never reach the proper channels responsible for maintaining the most current information.

Some companies have made the engineering process so complex with red-tape signatures and sign-offs that often the part is already in use before it has been totally approved. Because of slowness to approve a new or replacement component, often materials requirement planning (MRP) is not reflective of the new part or new level. When this happens, MRP continues to generate requirements for the incorrect level or part number unless a planner intervenes in the releasing process by changing the parameters to prevent reordering. Because the new components are being used and the old revision (or part) is not, MRP is still back-flushing inventory using the old part number, which may lead to a negative inventory in the system.

It is imperative that MRP reflect the change before a plant uses a new revision or new part number. If MRP is not changed, a manual effort will be required to follow the inventories of both the old part/revision and the new part/revision. This scenario is all too common in some companies, and it leads to some shortages and expedites.

GET IT CORRECT AT THE BEGINNING

Any bill of materials that is not 100 percent accurate in MRP may contribute to a part shortage in the future. Some plants and corporations are better at controlling the accuracy of the bills than others. Because bills of materials are input into MRP systems manually, errors can be made with usage and part numbers. It is often difficult for planners to notice such errors until it is too late and a plant shortage exists.

The best practice is for planners to investigate the reason for the shortage and then take immediate corrective action. Plants in the firefighting mode often overlooked this investigation because of time constraints; however, the problem generally recurs. If bills of materials accuracy is a primary contributor to the firefighting mode, executive management must address the issue. Simply verifying the bills of materials to a print or drawing customer or company supplied may not be sufficient to stop the inaccuracies.

A wise executive will invest time and personnel in ensuring that bills of materials are correct. The best practice is to review each bill of materials on record in MRP with the actual on-site application. There is no better method than to watch how a product is put together and check off the components actually used. Often what has been overlooked are the small parts or changes made on-site by engineers (who forget to change the record).

Sometimes manufacturing makes substitutions that never are conveyed to the engineering or materials department. This situation is often difficult if not impossible to correct.

DEVELOP GOOD SCRAP REPORTING METHODS

Plant departments that require the most accuracy often are partially responsible for the raging fire. Inaccurate scrap reporting can wreak havoc on any inventory system. In many companies, scrap reduction is a high priority, and accurate scrap reporting is not.

To some plants, it is more important to impress corporate with lower scrap numbers than are actually occurring. The pressure imposed on manufacturing managers to reduce scrap numbers generally induces them to overlook the importance reporting scrap accurately.

In order for the perpetual inventory to have a chance of being correct, manufacturing must take ownership for reporting scrap accurately. As long as manufacturing people are measured on scrap percentages, manufacturing has no real stake in ensuring scrap is reported correctly, and there will never be a consistent and accurate method of reporting scrap. Nothing that would negatively affect supervisors' performance is going to take precedence over the supervisor meeting the plant scrap goal.

Most plants record scrap using some paper reporting process. The basic issue with such a process is that it is prone to errors, in the form of incorrect part numbers or bills of materials level, or even in the amount reported because of the complexity of the part. If line workers are responsible for scrap reporting, workers may be reluctant to report the scrap out of fear of being reprimanded.

The very nature of the product being produced may complicate the ability to report the scrap accurately. When producing products that are difficult to report scrap on a part number basis, some companies use weight to measure the dollars of scrap. The problem with this method for inventory management is that there is no accurate posting of scrap by part number in the inventory system. The materials people must take frequent counts of materials and make manual adjustments in the computer system.

It is of no value to hire clerks to input incomplete or inaccurate scrap data into the MRP system. Executive management must review the scrap reporting process to determine the best practice. Because the best practice must consider the nature of the product being manufactured, different reporting methods may need to be constructed for a particular class of inventory.

In some processes, scrap reporting can be controlled by not allowing workers to dump materials into scrap bins arbitrarily. Some companies are able to lock down scrap reporting by placing scrap bins at the work-stations. The scrap is then counted at the end of the shift by an independent group and recorded properly into the system. However, even this process is not flawless.

OWNERSHIP OF INVENTORY

If manufacturing and materials control are to be measured effectively, there needs to be a clear division of ownership for the inventory and what becomes of it. Materials people can argue that once the materials are passed to the production floor, the inventory is subject to many unknowns beyond their control and inventory control should therefore become manufacturing's responsibility.

In most plants, the materials control personnel generally are held accountable for the inability of the manufacturing floor to protect and preserve the inventory. Since materials people are considered to be a service department, they are considered nonvalue added. The phrase "nonvalue added" is ludicrous and has no place in any conversation because there is value added in managing supply, quality, and engineering issues. Everyone in the organization contributes to the bottom-line profits, from the clerks to the chief executive officer.

Manufacturing is generally considered the most important department in the organization. To some executives, supporting departments do not make money and thus are not considered as important as manufacturing. "Important" becomes synonymous with "correct." thereby placing the onus for all inventory issues solely on materials control, even when manufacturing has loose inventory control practices that may contribute to inventory inaccuracies.

It is best to consider all supporting departments as essential in their contribution to the bottom line. Understanding the issues the supporting departments face and correcting inefficiencies can only help augment production efforts.

Ever since the concept of line-side storage took hold, there has been an increase in part shortages because the inventory is more difficult to control. No one would place a stack of $100 bills on a bar and walk away believing that it would be there when they returned. Likewise, no materials person believes that materials on the floor will be accounted for accurately.

To control materials accurately on the production floor, MRP must correctly reflect what is out there. If materials are missing in the factory (MRP work-in-process [WIP] location), there is only one alternative: Write it off to scrap.

VANISHING INVENTORY ISSUE

Most plants do not adopt the practice of writing off missing materials on the manufacturing floor to scrap. Instead, they use a cycle counting account to capture the shortfalls. At the end of the month, accounting lists the amount of cycle count adjustments on the ledger. This method of accounting generally means that materials control is managing the inventory badly.

If the parts are not there, then where did they go? This question may never be answered unless the methods of issuing materials to the floor are changed. Some materials departments complicate the issue of cycle counting adjustments by making frequent changes to inventory balances in the system. The accuracy of cycle counting is suspect when the materials department makes cyclical adjustments for a part number one day to the next.

When the missing inventory is written off to scrap, the plant as a whole suffers with the loss to the bottom line. The plant also suffers when cycle count adjustments result in inventory written off the books. Perhaps the pain of reporting missing inventory as scrap is the better alternative because everyone will scramble to fix the issues.

The answer to the missing inventory is difficult to resolve; however, simply writing materials off to a cycle count adjustment is not the answer, nor is simply scraping the missing materials. The answer is to instill best practices to make it difficult not to report scrap accurately and to make cycle count adjustments without investigation and permanent resolution.

Suppliers are the ones that end up feeling the pressure of ineffective scrap reporting systems or wild swings in cycle counting adjustments because it is reflected in their releases. When suppliers complain of vacillating releases, generally the cause is the company's inability to manage the inventory in the plant with a high degree of accuracy.

Customer release fluctuations are responsible for some of the changes in demand that trickle down to the releases. In most cases, however, these fluctuations are not the reason but an excuse. An executive who is made aware of supplier complaints concerning vacillating releases should investigate and resolve the inventory management issues.

Compounding the inability to control materials on the manufacturing floor and the possibility that there is a bill of materials issue is the inability of the materials department to manage the system parameters that govern how MRP interprets and displays information. Essential in any good materials system is the correct use of all planning parameters in the various modules that control the calculations for releasing materials.

In most companies, it is difficult to obtain any information that correctly depicts how to manage planning parameters. Manuals for the MRP system are often difficult to read and interpret or just not available. The reasoning behind each field in the MRP control modules is often a trial-and-error process of entering data in a field and then reviewing the outcome; however, trained materials people can work with the fields to obtain the desired results.

RESPONSIBILITY FOR INVENTORY: THE FEW OR THE MANY?

Answers to the inventory accuracy problem are often complicated by programs thought to improve inventory control but that actually impose control issues. Procedures and processes that allow anyone to access inventory and many people from various departments to access the inventory system for data input or output damage the integrity of inventory accuracy. It is almost impossible to expect the plant's entire workforce to manage the inventory properly.

Many companies allow workers to input the number of finished goods completed into the MRP system. Without a system of verification, this system is prone to errors that generally will result in finished goods inaccuracies. The best practice is to minimize manual entries by restricting the number of people who can enter data into the system. Even with one or two people managing the input of finished goods into the system, there needs to be a verification system to check the accuracy of the input. Chapter 20 describes a best practice method that is almost perfect for reporting finished goods.

With inventory accuracy and control dependent on perfect input, perfect output, and perfect setting of planning parameters, if the result is negative, then the fire starts in materials and continues to burn brightly. The problems continue to fester until the entire systems breaks down. When the entire system breaks down, some managers employ stock chasers and expediters. These are simply stopgap measures that do nothing to correct the situation.

A company that has a group of people who spend most of their time chasing and expediting materials into and out of the plant has reached the very bottom level of materials control. At this point, it is difficult to change the process and the thinking of the plant.

The only way to stop firefighting is to employ a materials control specialist familiar with the MRP processes. This person must keep from being sucked into the mainstream problems of the plant and must focus entirely on reversing the process of firefighting.

Firefighting can eliminated only if the plant manager and the plant staff are totally committed to keeping the independent manager focused on correcting the problems.

CHAPTER 4

A STRONG, WELL-BALANCED MATERIALS ORGANIZATION

MATERIALS MANAGEMENT STATUS IN ORGANIZATIONS

In many companies, materials control is the least respected and most misunderstood department. Its reputation is related directly to the success of the systems it attempts to control.

Attention usually is drawn to the materials department when major issues arise with part shortages, nondelivery to the customer, excess freight, and physical inventory losses. Although not all issues are related directly to the materials function and control, materials people are expected to control the inventory levels despite issues that are out of their control.

The wide differences in salaries paid for materials managers is an indication of the degree of authority and responsibility that the company places on this effort. Companies at the lowest end of the pay scale are likely to believe that materials management is a purely clerical activity and that virtually anyone is capable of managing the system. Companies at the high end of the pay scale are serious about controlling and managing inventory accuracy, and the associated costs.

OBSTACLES PREVENTING MATERIALS MANAGEMENT SUCCESS

The reasons for part shortages and other inefficiencies may not be the computer system itself but rather either the lack or inaccuracy of data being entered into the system. All computer-controlled inventory systems will fail if the information entered and taken out is not accurate. The data input from receiving, shipping, and all processes that affect the inventory balance must be managed properly so that errors become a minor issue. At a minimum, any manual input or output system must be verified for accuracy.

The parameters used in the computer system to govern materials requirement planning (MRP) must be correct in order to generate accurate and consistent information for the plant and the suppliers. Materials people must understand how best to utilize planning parameters to obtain the results they are seeking.

In principle, MRP works the same in any software package. Software packages differ in software complexity and in the placement, coding, and impact that a particular planning parameter has on the inventory. Planning parameters are an integral part of materials operations; they are discussed in more detail in Chapter 10.

As mentioned earlier, excess freight expenses are one major concern for companies. If a plant is not meeting expectations for managing excess freight, poor planning, computer system problems, or other plant management issues may be generating hidden problems.

Computer system glitches are not that common, although they can occur in the software or when the system crashes. In any system crash caused by a power outage, power surge, or software glitch, there is generally a loss of data. Sometimes the information systems department is able to recover the lost data; other times it is necessary to revert to a time before the crash and reenter all information from that point on—a painstaking effort, especially if there is no clear trail of what was being entered into the system at the time of the crash.

Blaming part shortages on customer schedule changes is generally shortsighted. Customers, especially original equipment manufacturers (OEMs), generally build product with a level schedule. (The only exception is for component parts that are optional or additional to their processes.) OEMs and most other manufacturing companies build the same amount of product every day for a simple reason: A level schedule is more productive and efficient than a fluctuating one.

OEMs also know when they are planning to add hours to their schedules or when they require Saturday production. Many OEMs maintain Web sites where the information for future production can be retrieved. Management should review this information weekly to determine the OEM run times and quantities.

The materials department also needs to review the long-term OEM scheduled production reports on the Web. Many times a plant is unprepared for surges in demand from the customer because the materials department has not interpreted the long-term releases correctly, or someone makes a conscious decision that the future release information is incorrect, even though it is not.

Communication with the customer is essential to avert long-term releasing issues that will eventually become tomorrow's releases if the customer suddenly requires more material and decides to move the shipping requirement date ahead. Customer releases are not always perfect, but customers are always right, especially if the release generation is within the quoted production agreement amount. Frequent visits by materials management personnel to customers are essential in averting releasing issues. It is to the advantage of the plant and the company to understand customers' production capabilities and output plans firsthand.

Communication and the ability to work with all support departments are crucial for successful materials management. Materials people need to stay involved with key decisions that can directly affect materials supply.

The accounting manager and the materials manager need to review the plant's excess freight issues carefully to ensure that the freight dollars spent are for the correct reasons. A large amount of excess freight expense attributed to a shortage of parts for the manufacturing process is a sign that planning process methods need to be reviewed. How many cases of excess freight expenses arise in a month that can be attributed to valid reasons? How many are most likely caused by inventory system mismanagement?

If a customer increases demand on short notice, the plant may accrue some excess freight charges in order to obtain components from suppliers. In this case, the customer should be paying for the excess freight.

Quality issues in a plant that result in a high frequency of downtime may create a supply issue to the customer. If a quality issue is affecting the entire product manufactured, the plant may have to devote itself to making exactly what the customer needs for a certain time. The materials department must follow customer releases and customer build schedules to ensure that the plant makes the correct parts to keep the customer supplied. Whenever a plant is in a critical supply mode, a well-balanced materials organization is needed to minimize the damage to the customer.

Another key management responsibility of a good materials organization is to reduce and manage the inventory to the lowest possible levels without hindering production. It takes exceptional planning, high inventory accuracy, and proper MRP system maintenance to lower inventories. In addition, ensuring that materials purchased are consumed as planned requires a high rate of machine uptime, low scrap rates, and high labor efficiencies.

At times the way in which the plant manages production can contribute to shortages. If the plant is building assemblies that are not released by the planning department, plant-induced shortages may arise. Sometimes plant management makes a decision to overrun assemblies in an effort to keep people busy; other times there may be an uptime issue on one part of the assembly process, and workers are moved elsewhere temporarily.

In many cases, the movement of workers from one assembly process to another is inefficient because the shifted workers are not fully trained. Often people do not want to be relocated to a job they are not comfortable with, and this alone causes some quality issues. Care must be taken for processes with a high fallout rate where technical skills are required. The scrap rate may soar with untrained workers on the job.

What are the plant's customer supplier ratings? If the grades are below par, what is the root cause? The answer lies in reviewing the grade information provided by all OEM and non-OEM customers carefully. Looking into the root causes may provide some surprising answers. Many materials departments have no real understanding of customer grading systems. It is important for the materials department to understand what is required to maintain a high customer grade. Web-based customer systems have evolved over the years into large, complex systems that are time consuming to manage for any plant. Dedicated people are required to manage the customer systems effectively; such management should not be taken lightly. Turnover in materials control staff is generally a high contributor to faltering grades, since new hires face the challenge of learning customers' Web-based systems.

It takes a strong materials department with an extensive knowledge of the inventory control system coupled with the ability to determine root cause, analyze and resolve issues, and put in place permanent corrective actions to effectively manage material control. The formula for material control success can be described in a simple statement: The selection of personnel and the training level required to manage the inventory is directly related to days of inventory, excess freight expenses, and amount of shortages in a plant.

Excellence in materials personnel and understanding how to manage the system and the perpetual inventory will always result in the lowest numbers in inventory, lowest excess freight charges, and fewest stock outages, provided all other plant processes are in control.

MEASURING MATERIALS MANAGEMENT SUCCESS

The success of the materials control department can be measured simply by adding together the excess freight costs, plus the downtime costs, plus the inventory losses (both physical and cycle counted), and dividing that sum by the salaries of the materials department personnel.

The resulting number is the excess cost of controlling materials. For example, if six salaries in the department are equal to a total of $360,000 and there was $2.5 million in excess costs related to materials control, then the cost of materials is $6.94 per dollar of salary paid to these employees. Of course, the ideal amount per salary dollar paid is zero; however, this amount may be unrealistic since there is always a chance that something will occur out of the ordinary, which will result in expedited freight.

With so much riding on the bottom line in companies today, executives need to place a high emphasis on obtaining a strong materials department with good leadership that will get the expected results. Materials control is a specialty, and those with experience can contribute immensely to the organization's objectives.

If the inventory dollars, customer delivery, and excess freight are not at the levels expected by top management, it is time to hire leaders with the strengths required to obtain the desired results. Concern for the control required must be balanced carefully with the personnel selected to lead the way. If we desire the lowest inventories, the best customer service, and the least amount of freight expenses, we need to focus on those objectives.

With the correct leadership and support from upper management, a strong and well-supported materials organization will attain the desired results. The first step for us to understand is the level of material control we believe we have in our organization. To do so, we must audit the practices of the materials department. The second step is to seek out experts in all areas of materials management and use their talents properly. Before selecting the proper materials team or team leadership, executives need to understand the principles behind a well-balanced materials organization. The next chapters explain the materials process and present a well-balanced materials organization.

CHAPTER 5

GENERAL REVIEW OF MATERIALS PRACTICES

Inventory is normally measured in total dollars, inventory days on hand, or turns. Although top managers usually prefer inventory to be stated in turns, most materials professionals prefer to speak in terms of inventory days on hand.

CALCULATING INVENTORY TURNS

There is no industry standard method of calculating the number of inventory turns. Because there is no consistency in calculating inventory turns, it is difficult to make comparisons that make sense. The lack of consistency in calculating turns stems from the data used by the accounting department. Some companies use next month's estimated sales in calculating inventory turns; others use the current month's sales. Some companies count in-transit materials; others do not.

Using the estimated sales numbers for the next month is justified because the inventory on hand has been purchased for the next month's sales. Materials people and plant managers prefer this calculation because when sales dollars are overstated for the next month, the inventory turns are lower than reality. The better method of calculating inventory turns is to use past sales dollars so that there is no way to fudge the numbers.

Usually inventory categories are broken down into five parts:

1. Finished goods
2. Work in process (WIP)
3. Raw materials
4. In-transit
5. Obsolete or inactive

The total inventory dollars broken down into these major categories is important to understanding and identifying any apparent issues. If one class of inventory is out of control, a thorough investigation is necessary to understand and correct the issues causing the imbalance. The proper mix of material dollars in each inventory category is directly related to the type of manufacturing. Some plants are WIP intensive, while others can maintain a one-piece process flow. The ultimate goal of all manufacturing should be to strive toward consistent manufacturing with one-piece flow. Companies that produce the same product every day should be able to accommodate consistent stable flow through the plant. Job shops where many of different products are manufactured in small quantities may never be able to attain one-piece flow because of part complexity and amount required.

OBSOLETE DOLLARS CALCULATED
IN INVENTORY TURNS

The amount of obsolete dollars in inventory is a factor that may prevent a plant from attaining its inventory goals. Many plants are reluctant to present the total dollar amount of obsolete material since this is a direct reflection on how well the plant is managed, and obsolescence directly affects the profit margins. Consequently, many materials organizations are faced with unrealistic inventory reduction goals that will never be attained.

Companies with a large dollar amount of obsolete material obsolescence should adjust the inventory target goal by all or a portion of the obsolete dollar amount. The goal of any plant should be to state accurately the inventory dollars to slow-moving and obsolete materials.

Carrying obsolete inventory on the books is an issue that may or may not face your company. Some companies have little or no obsolescence; others have much more that they can write off without causing a lot of top-level attention to the problem.

How obsolete inventory that cannot possibly be used is built up in inventory is anyone's guess. Some materials departments are better at controlling engineering changes. Customer balance-outs and poor control may be the issue. Sometimes sales or engineering changes that must be incorporated immediately are the reason for obsolescences. Ultimately, there is no excuse for carrying junk on the books.

Executives managing the company must understand the impact of a sudden engineering change that will render components obsolete. If an engineering change is customer driven, the customer should be notified in writing that there is an obsolescence cost. The customer should agree to pay for any obsolescence incurred by the engineering change. If the company is responsible for an immediate engineering change, the plant controller should set up an accrual account for the impending obsolescence dollars and write it off.

The best practice for avoiding a buildup of slow-moving or obsolete inventory is for the accounting department to generate an aging report that shows the days of inventory by part number. Inventory that is aged beyond an acceptable number of days without activity or little activity needs to be tracked back to the root cause. Once the root cause is determined, the company needs to create a proactive action plan to prevent the problem from arising in the future.

A buildup of obsolescence is often the result of a plant not wanting to show a loss with a write-down of inventory. It is too easy to carry the obsolescence on the ledger as good material. A good materials manager makes a point of revealing the obsolescent portion of the inventory when preparing inventory graphs. A better materials manager is able to prevent the buildup of obsolescence.

As long as a product evolves and changes, some obsolescence may not be able to be avoided. The annual plant budget should include a reasonable amount for obsolescence. Good controllers can accrue the cash required to write off the obsolete inventory. Not to allow for any inventory write-down simply hides a problem in the plant; eventually it will cost someone's job. The dollar amount reserved for obsolescence will vary from industry to industry; however, there should be enough historical data in the company to prepare a benchmark. Companies that do not accrue for obsolescence are just kidding themselves.

CUSTOMER-GENERATED OBSOLESCENCE

A facility should never accept obsolescence generated by customer change. There is no reason to let a customer change a product or process without paying for the inventory that will become obsolete. A good materials department will know how to avoid being saddled with inventory resulting from a customer change. A good customer contract has provisions for inventory that was purchased in good faith and is no longer required by the customer.

Often corporations do not have a complete understanding of customers' obsolescence guidelines. Some customers place a timetable to complete a claim for obsolescence. If the timetable is not met, then the plant owns the materials.

Sometimes components from the plant's supplier base contain lead times that extend beyond the customer's allowed days. Any components that the plant purchases that have long supplier lead times should be explained to the customer up front. It is important to write these components into the contract to protect the supplier and the plant from absorbing the inventory loss. For example, say the customer generates a production schedule that extends 12 months. If the plant uses a supplier that requires 20 weeks of lead time, this can result in an obsolescence dispute. The best way to avoid disputes with customers is to make all cases of long lead times part of the sales contract.

OBSOLESCENCE CONTROLS

Obsolete inventory that is allowed to build up without any plan to scrap, rework or sell the excess reserve serves no purpose other than to overstate a company's total assets. A bad scenario occurs when the company's sale results in the acquirer inheriting a large amount of obsolete material, a situation that happens too often.

If there is a major issue with obsolescence, there most likely is a major issue with the planning for balance-outs (ending the life of a project, part number, or part level). Materials requirement planning (MRP) systems are simply not capable of phasing out inventory without human intervention. Planners must be able to manage the balance-out of materials so there is no cost to the company. As easy as it may sound, phasing out inventory is no easy task. Doing so depends on the ability to finalize customer demand and maintain the accuracy of the perpetual inventory.

Most MRP systems have parameters that can turn off the backflushing of a component at a specific date and at the same time kick in a new level or part number. The danger in using this parameter arises when the part usage is extended. If someone in materials overlooks changing the end date, there will be no new releases to the supply base and a high probability of a shortage.

The most common mistakes are not getting a balance-out number from the customer in writing and not having a good count on the materials on hand. People responsible for a balance-out of materials need to ensure that the perpetual inventory is correct and that the amount of WIP is controlled.

Many companies no longer track WIP in MRP, which makes tracking WIP difficult. Uncontrolled WIP essentially means that the materials department must be able to break down the subassemblies into raw components during cycle counting to ensure that the perpetual inventory is correct. In addition, the planner needs to be aware of any inventory that may be in a service area, rework area, quality hold area, or distributed throughout several production areas.

A strong materials department works with manufacturing to limit the amount of subassembly work when nearing a phase-out date or target quantity and ensures that suppliers are aware of the phasing out of materials. It is the responsibility of the materials department to issue in writing the final numbers to suppliers. Suppliers that receive final balance-out numbers will be able to charge the plant only for those materials they have been authorized make.

Too many organizations fail to manage the supply base for the final balance-out. The result can be shocking when the supplier ships large quantities of materials during or after a final production run. Resolving a dispute with a supplier that has excess materials is not an easy task, especially when the supplier is a sole source of the materials. The supplier can and will hold shipments of new products hostage for payment of obsolescence. Generally, the plant loses and pays for the materials.

It is equally important to manage part level changes to minimize obsolescence. Level changes come in two forms: a stated end date and a rolling change date end date. The rolling change allows the plant to use all of the material at the current level before launching the next level. The materials department must be aware of what is on hand for the part that is being replaced and must ensure that manufacturing does not inadvertently use the newer part before the old part is consumed.

The best practice is for a plant to have a locked area where new parts or nonapproved materials are stored. In an environment where engineering changes are critical, it is especially important not to accidentally release unapproved materials to the manufacturing floor. The manufacturing floor must never implement new engineering changes without consulting materials management.

A large amount of WIP is not a good sign that the manufacturing process is using best practices to minimize inventory and gain the benefits of one-piece flow. (This concept does not apply to job shops that make one-of-a-kind products with many variations.) The more inventory on the manufacturing floor in WIP, the more difficult it is to manage the inventory accurately. Minimizing WIP is the best practice for proper inventory management.

A large amount of finished goods, without a clear reason, is usually a sign of machining and production issues that must be addressed. Plants usually carry large finished goods inventories to protect themselves from short shipping due to internal issues. The only valid reason for carrying excess finished goods is a bank build for a pending engineering change.

Machine uptime or labor problems may create the need for excess finished goods inventory. Executives need to focus on how to resolve these issues.

In today's operational environment, capital budgets reductions for plants are common. Many plants are forced to keep equipment running beyond its intended life, which usually results in excessive downtime.

The smart executive is able to show top management the costs of maintaining antiquated equipment versus purchasing new equipment by capturing all of the associated costs. Even if an executive can show a cost savings in the long term, many corporate chief executive officers (CEOs) continue to focus on short-term profits. This problem is compounded by those companies that have a high CEO turnover rate because the short-term CEO wants to control costs. The short-term profit concept works only until the equipment finally expires and quits functioning altogether.

There may be a specific need to carry a larger-than-normal finished goods inventory because of customer fluctuations or a pending level change—a new revision to an existing product—that requires the equipment to be altered. The astute materials manager will generate a finished goods inventory report that shows the normal inventory levels and the level that needs to be carried to support changes or fluctuating customer demand.

Generally, a 2-day–1-day–2-day split of finished goods, WIP, and raw materials is the best practice and target; however, not too many plants can obtain the goal of five days of inventory, because they have not implemented industry best practices.

Companies that produce multiple variations of products may need to change the mix of inventory to a 2-day–2-day–1-day split of inventory, assuming the finished product can be made readily from the WIP.

The advent of one-piece flow concepts eliminated the tracking of WIP. Some companies are better at one-piece flow, due either to the nature of the product or the nature of process that has been developed. Companies with a high amount of WIP because of the nature of the product should add WIP pay points in the bills of materials.

Many companies today regard what little WIP they have as raw materials until the final product is reported in the system. This practice, and the practice of keeping the inventory at finished goods level, is sound only if there is not a large amount of WIP in the plant or a large number of products that use the same component. Shortages can and will occur if there are multiple usages of a component on items with a heavy WIP inventory that is not tracked by computer.

Most WIP overbuild is generated from having too much labor or having a process that is not continuous because of machine uptime or labor constraints. If a process requires more WIP than normal, it may be necessary to track the WIP in MRP as a subassembly so that the raw materials are reduced from inventory properly and new releases are generated to the supply base on a timely basis.

Some manufacturing people fail to understand that the MRP system is designed to generate orders based on the inventory on hand. If there is a large amount of unreported WIP, the inventory of each component used in the subassembly will be overstated as available raw material. A component that is used in multiple assemblies is especially vulnerable to shortages when one item is stockpiled.

There is a method to reduce from inventory the raw materials at the WIP level. Some companies transfer the components from point-of-use racks to WIP with a scanning process that automatically changes the location of the components on hand. The component releasing process is then set up to order replacements based on the inventory in both areas.

Attempting to control WIP by moving the inventory from one location to another is not without its problems. If the lack of scrap reporting or quality issues are prevalent, the WIP inventory may be overstated on the books, resulting in an inventory shrink when a physical inventory is taken.

Finished goods inventory levels depend on the nature of the business and customer demands. It is advisable to carry the finished goods inventory at a level that will maintain customers' requirements, plus any minor fluctuations in demand. Generally, the amount of finished goods should equate to the plant's ability to make a predetermined scheduled shipment amount, plus the amount of production that a customer might use on a weekend. Based on this strategy, the plant would work the same Saturday or the Saturday after the one the customer worked in order to replace the inventory shipped.

The best manufacturing philosophy follows a simple rule: The plant or cell to reach peak efficiency should manufacture products for the customer at the same rate the customer is using the products, or work the same hours as the customer, or stop production when the customer's daily demand is met.

Too many plants use customer downtime to shift their workers to other areas, where they usually are not as effective or efficient. Other plants use the time to perform preventive maintenance (PM), which should already have been factored into the daily production routine.

PM is something that many plants find is near impossible to control. The root cause of not being able to complete PM on a regular schedule is the inability to manufacture product to the efficiency levels required. It is imperative that plants accept or modify the manufacturing rates imposed on them by corporate before those rates become permanent.

Corporate errors regarding run rates always spill into the plant and become a plant issue. Some plants are able to improve production efficiencies with lean[1] events that compensate for overstated production rates. At times it is nearly impossible to meet corporate-established manufacturing run rates. This is why the plant input is essential in determining how much product can be made in an hour.

One misconception in many plants is that safety stock or bank levels[2] must be maintained at all costs. Supervisors may want to replace safety stock immediately by scheduling day/evening or weekend overtime. Bank stock covers fluctuations in demand from the customer or manufacturing/quality issues that may arise in the plant. Once the extra inventory is shipped, an action plan to replace it should be agreed on, but running the plant in an overtime mode without a recovery plan does not make sense, especially when the components to replenish the bank are not on order. Sometimes a plant can afford to delay replacing the bank based on a customer's scheduled downtime day. This plan makes more sense than generating overtime hours.

The number of days that should be considered as the minimum for inventory in a plant is directly related the locations of suppliers from whom the materials are purchased. If purchases are overseas, the usual in-transit time is equal to the travel time of the vessel, plus the time it takes to clear customs and move the product to the using plant.

Upper management may believe that inventory should always be at a certain level, no matter where the materials are purchased. This is simply not true, since overseas procurements will require more of a hedge to protect against product delay due to a late vessel arrival or incomplete paperwork that delays customs clearance. In addition, if a quality issue should arise with a recent shipment, then the plant would not have much material to fall back on. No one likes air freight expenses from foreign countries, especially if the product shipped is bulky and heavy.

Another misconception is that vessels can arrive weekly; thus there is no need to increase the inventory. Although ships can indeed arrive weekly, a cost must be realized. It is in the best interests of the company to fill a container so that costs are minimized. Sharing a container is not always the best option for a company; if the container is on hold because of an issue unrelated to the plant, the plant will not be able to obtain the materials until the issue is resolved.

Materials departments that do not recognize the need to carry more inventories for overseas-sourced components can expect to pay premium freight dollars. The cost of one premium freight shipment from an overseas supplier might negate all of the savings that were expected.

A simple calculation can be used to determine the level inventory and the number of days it should be carried when portions of the inventory are domestic and portions are international. The calculation is to multiply the percentage of international dollars used in the product times the average cost of goods sold; for example, if 60 percent of the purchased components are international in a total purchased cost of $900,000, then $540,000 is the cost for international components and $360,000 is the cost for domestic components. From these numbers, a days-on-hand target can be developed that is reasonable for the plant. It may be best for the plant to show the days on hand for domestic components separate from the days on hand for foreign-sourced components in graph format.

Here is an example of calculating the inventory that a plant should carry with both international and domestic suppliers. From the previous example, 1 average day of inventory is equal to $31,578. Multiply the $31,578 by the inventory goal for domestic inventory of 5 days. Then multiply the product times 40 percent for the domestic purchase cost of the product for a dollar amount of $63,158. Multiply the international target of 24 days by the average day of inventory of $31,758. Then multiply this number by 60 percent for a result of $454,737. Adding the $63,158 to the $454,737, the result is $517,895. The plant should be carrying $517,895 in inventory as a goal. The result of this example is 16.4 days of inventory (the $517,895 of total inventory value divided by the $31,578).

In some cases, there may be three parts to the inventory calculation depending on where the plant is located. Mexico, for example, may purchase some material domestically, some from the United States, and some from Europe. The lead time in this case might be 7 days as opposed to 3 domestically and 10 or more days internationally.

WHAT ARE THE CUSTOMER RATINGS?

There may or may not be a formal rating system for nonoriginal equipment manufacturers (non-OEMs). The OEM customer ratings are comprised of delivery, quality, and communication levels. The non-OEM rating is not clearly defined and it may be simple or complex based entirely by the customers expectations. If the customer does not have a rating system, then a self-rating system needs to be developed. The self-rating system is generated by the materials department and it needs to be based on the number of parts or shipments that were shipped to the customer orders on-time.

A simple measurement is the total number of shipments divided by the number of shipments sent on time. Some executives insist on using the number of line items shipped on time as the measurement. Although this has some credence and is more reflective of the actual on-time delivery, gathering the information by line item is generally too time consuming.

It serves no purpose to calculate customer on-time delivery that is not agreed on with the customer; therefore, a plant should show any calculation to the customer. It is better to avoid showing top management a plant calculation that shows a high delivery rating from a customer when that customer is complaining about the delivery.

OEM delivery ratings often include parts that are not in the immediate control of the materials department. Unfortunately, the materials department is often held responsible for the entire customer score for the ratings, even if there are extenuating circumstances beyond its control.

The OEM grade should be broken down to show all of the areas graded, which indicates the areas that need improvement. Generally, the grade can be broken into three parts: (1) materials control influence with timeliness and maintenance, (2) on-time shipments, and (3) quality issues. Quality issues can destroy a customer rating to the point that it is impossible to reverse, even though the materials were delivered on time. Once poor quality negatively impacts a grade, it is impossible to improve the grade because most suppliers consider this area as most critical.

The number of different customer systems that must be managed when placing business into a plant must be considered. Staffing becomes an issue when there are a number of different complex and time-consuming customer systems to manage. The Ford and Chrysler systems are high maintenance; specific time schedules are set for reviewing and updating their Internet-based control systems.

If customer grades are low in the maintenance categories, there usually is either a training issue or the person assigned to manage the log-in times has many other functions that may take precedence. In order to properly handle and staff the various customer systems, the time required to manage the systems properly must be assessed.

HOW DOES THE SHIPPING DEPARTMENT FUNCTION?

Discipline and proper procedures are crucial in the maintenance of a well-rounded shipping department. First, there is the need to understand how the shipping data is retrieved. Most customers today transmit electronic releases that are imported into the company's computer system. The information systems department has the responsibility to provide the system interpretation of the electronic releases transmitted by the customer, simply known as electronic data interchange (EDI). Customers' electronic releases may be daily or weekly along with a planning forecast that may extend out as far as a year or more.

The complexity of retrieving and analyzing releases from the MRP system usually determines who is responsible for generating the customer requirements for shipments. The more complex customer releases are, the more there may be a need for a specialist who can analyze the releases and determine what should be shipped for the day and when.

Errors that need to be addressed may show on the EDI transmission. If the link between the customer part number and the plant part number is not correct, the system will reject the releases. All errors on the EDI error report should be addressed immediately.

Customer-generated errors are the customer's responsibility to correct. Until it does so, the error will continue to show on the log and may even generate releases for inactive products and components. This is a common issue in the automotive sector. One method of resolving the issue at the plant level is to deactivate the part number that the customer is incorrectly transmitting.

Cumulative balances[3] for shipments the customer sends must match the cumulative balances that the plant has recorded. Cumulative balances must be correct in order for the plant to print the correct shipping schedule. If the plant shows a higher cumulative balance shipped than the customer shows, the shipments will be understated. If the plant shows a lower accumulative balance, shipment will occur.

Someone in the materials organization should manage cumulative balances on a daily basis and as a primary task. Managing cumulative balances is a matter of comparing the in-house MRP system cumulative balance to that of the customer and then making the appropriate changes in the system.

Some customers may send a log of all the cumulative discrepancies via EDI. Some MRP systems can print reports showing the differences in cumulative balances. Cumulative balances that show discrepancies in shipping totals need to be corrected before printing a shipping schedule or making an actual shipment to the customer. It is in the best interests of the plant to have a dedicated person or department responsible for correcting shipping balances.

There is a need to ensure that the data the OEM is transmitting is received properly into the plant's MRP system. Data files in all systems must contain the correct information in order to read the customer releases properly. If there are incorrect parameters in linking the customer's part number to the company's, releases may come into the plant incorrectly or not at all. The plant's data files must be linked properly to the customers' transmitted files in order to obtain the correct release information. A system-generated report must show the fallout of customer releases due to a variety of interface problems that need to be corrected. The error report is usually printed after the EDI has been received from the customer. This report contains data that must be reviewed carefully and corrected in order for the releases to be received properly. Chapter 11 is devoted to EDI.

Customers generally transmit via EDI the number of units or quantity required to ship. The plant computer system translates the customer data into a format that the plant can read. For example, the raw data electronically sent may be converted into standard packages or a ship pattern, depending on the agreement with the customer and the way in which the plant parameters in the system are set up.

It is important to understand customer needs and then set the parameters for data interpretation to those needs. A failure to set the correct package quantity, for example, may result in shipping products that contain less than standard packages. It is important to set the standard package with the customer in the initial purchase order contract so that the customer will generate releases in multiples of standard packages; otherwise the plant will spend valuable time packing small quantities of materials or changing the releases manually to reflect the actual customer need.

When customers are responsible for the freight and for tracking product when it leaves the plant, they normally designate their carrier of choice. When a plant decides to use a carrier other than the one specified by the customer, the liability for the load no longer lies with the customer but with the plant. If the carrier fails to meet the delivery time or a catastrophic event occurs, this can have devastating effects.

Using a carrier other than the customer-specified carrier might result in air charters costing thousands of dollars because the nonapproved carrier fails to deliver. The problem can be avoided by using the correct carrier assigned by the customer. If there is an issue with the customer's selected carrier, the customer or designated logistics company should assign another carrier. Many companies use a logistics company that will assign alternate carriers if required. No company should accept responsibility for the customer's product once ownership passes to the customer using their assigned carrier. It is wiser for the plant to incur the expedited freight costs of the carrier selected by the customer than to attempt to avoid extra costs by using an alternate carrier of the plant's choice.

A well-managed shipping department will have a verification system in effect to ensure that the advanced notice (ASN)[4] and shipper have been properly transmitted. If any error has been detected, the transaction can be reversed and corrected before the customer receives the materials in its plant. The OEM customer generally allows a period during which corrections can be made to the ASN before a penalty is assessed. Ford and Chrysler have sophisticated Internet systems that allow senders to correct the ASN online within a specified time.

Of all the releasing systems available, the most difficult to manage is the facsimile system. Customers that use the facsimile systems generally do not have a good release management system. The problem with paper releases is that the demand is often over- or understated, or there is a delay in receiving newer releases. Mistakes are more likely to occur with a manual system since there is a risk of not receiving the releases on time or misinterpreting the actual amount on order, given what is in transit.

In addition, paper releases received once per week are not generated in real time; therefore, the customer may call to stop or increase a shipment without notice. The paper release drives the plant to carry more finished goods than normal in order to protect against sudden customer increases. Paper releases offer no guarantee of stability. The company needs to have a complete understanding with the customer regarding the management of engineering changes.

The supplying plant is responsible for entering the paper releases correctly into the computer system to drive its manufacturing and shipping requirements. Tracking cumulative balances is the most common issue with the paper system. Both parties should review the cumulative balances on a regular basis so that there is agreement on the balance shipped.

All shipping departments must maintain shipping guides for each customer's requirements so that the information is available for those who may need to ship product under unusual circumstances. The shipping guides should be arranged by customer and located where shipping is performed. Well-defined shipping guides should contain examples of how to handle just about every situation that would occur in a customer's shipment. Phone listings for trucking companies and customer contacts must be readily accessible so that when an issue arises, the customer can be contacted easily. The standard carrier alpha code (SCAC) should be posted visibly, in case the normal carrier is brokered to another carrier with an unfamiliar SCAC code. The plant must transmit the SCAC code in the ASN so that the customer can track the carrier hauling the freight. Failure to use the correct SCAC code will make it difficult if not impossible for customers to determine the status of the shipment.

Personnel responsible for shipments must be properly trained. A well-trained staff will prevent many common errors.

Some customers that maintain supplier grades electronically are excellent at reporting the issues that arise with shipping. A review of the types of shipping violations is a clue to what type of training is necessary to avoid a recurrence of the issue. Often plants allow shipping problems to continue without seeking understand how to correct the issue. The best practice is to ensure that someone in the materials group is well versed in customers' shipping policies and procedures.

HOW DOES THE RECEIVING DEPARTMENT FUNCTION?

Proper receiving policies and procedures are an important part of the success of material systems. A backlog of components that are waiting to be released in receiving creates confusion and frustration for materials personnel, who need to know when materials have arrived and where they are located. The best practice is to set a policy of entering all receipts into the system within an hour of the receipt or, at minimum, by the end of each day.

Most MRP systems will accommodate a quality inspection location that is managed in the materials system which can be used when receiving incoming materials. The inspection location should be used only if the incoming materials need to be verified every time they are received.

When random inspections are the policy, an inspection location is an added, unnecessary movement. An inspection location also adds to the audit function of materials management. Often people forget to transfer the components from the inspection location to the stock location. Nevertheless, if components must be inspected, they should be verified on a timely basis.

All products received should be delivered to the point-of-use area or storeroom within a few hours after being received so that the plant staff does not waste time searching for materials.

If a plant has off-shift production, problems arise when there is no one available to release materials from quality inspection are required to keep manufacturing going. This leads to second-shift workers making some decisions that may turn out to be incorrect. A component may be used that should not have been used, or the manager may decide to shut the line down for a lack of a component that would have been normally released on the day shift.

Executives can use a quick tour of the area to review the receiving process. Such a tour may reveal some surprising issues and raise some pertinent questions. For example, how much of the previous day's inventory has been recorded into the system and placed in the proper locations? If the answer is less than 100 percent, there are issues that must be addressed to correct the failure to move materials quickly.

There may be materials in receiving with hold tags that are several weeks or even months old. The longer materials remain on hold, the less chance that the supplier and the plant will resolve the quality issue. If components have a shelf life and they are placed on hold, a delay in a resolution of conformance issues may result in the plant absorbing the loss.

The lack of timely inspections or noninspection approval presents confusion and often a loss of lot tractability that is required by some customers in order to trace a potential defective part back to the lowest raw material used in their manufacturing process. Lack of timely inspection may lead to plant personnel taking components from the quality area without the final processing in order to keep the manufacturing lines operating. The result could be a high rejection rate and a costly sort if a problem arises with the quality of the part that was not released through the proper process.

If product is backed up waiting for inspection approval, a review of the inspection process is necessary to determine the root cause and provide a reasonable solution. Implementing a process of skip-lot management is a necessity for moving materials from point of receipt to the rack or floor locations in a timely manner. Skip-lot inspection requires that suppliers become self-certified with the products they are providing so that only random shipments are reviewed by quality. Self-certified suppliers usually provide the self-certification information along with the product that informs the quality control department that the product received has passed quality self certification standards. The plant inspection department still must review these documents in order to conclude that the material meets specifications before the product is released production.

The best method for moving components through the receiving process is with a skip-lot computer-generated bar coding system. The skip-lot program is designed to suppress label printing for items that *require* inspection. The suppression of the printing of inspection labels can help prevent the taking of components that are not approved for production. This subject is discussed in more detail in Chapter 20.

NOTES

1. "Lean" is a buzzword for streamlining a production process.
2. The term "bank levels" is used for materials that are stored for pending engineering changes.
3. Cumulative balances—Each time a shipment is made electronically, the total ship quantity for the year is increased by that amount.
4. An ASN is sent electronically to inform the customer that a shipment has been made.

CHAPTER 6

LEAD TIME

What is lead time? The traditional interpretation of "lead time" for components is the total time it takes a supplier to procure raw material, manufacture the product, ship, and for the receiving plant to receive it. Today the traditional version of lead time applies only to new products that have never been produced by a supplier or if raw materials, dies, tools, and/or the process for making product are new. It also applies to some long lead times.

Today the phrase "lead time" is synonymous with "transit time," which refers only to the time it takes to move product from the supplier to the customer.

Carrier selection controls transit time. There are three types of freight carriers: expediters, full truckload, and less than truckload. The quickest method of shipping product is via an expedited carrier, and there are numerous services with a vast number of price ranges. Full-truck and less-than-truckload carriers may have identical lead times.

Since "lead time" means "transit time," the materials group must make some allowances to protect against missed deliveries by adding safety stock. One method can be used to increase the release quantity. This method is to add into materials requirements planning (MRP) a safety stock number that calculates the amount of stock to carry for a set period. Depending on the nature of the product, the reliability of the supply base, and the distance to the plant, materials management can assign the proper values for safety stock.

In best-in-class operations, suppliers are expected to ship materials to a pull signal or electronic data interchange–released pull signal, in which the shortest time equals the time it takes to ship the product to the customer. A company is considered to be applying best-in-class manufacturing techniques when product can be shipped on a specific day with the correct quantity as specified by customer releases. Generally, there may be several authorized shipping releases and ship dates; however, the only release that is considered firm is the release that is due to ship on a particular day.

In addition to the daily release schedule, suppliers receive weekly, monthly, and annual forecasts from customers. The total forecast from customers should exceed the time it takes the entire supply chain to purchase raw materials and manufacture the needed component.

Plants use monthly forecasts primarily to project labor and capacity requirements in the short term.

The farther out the release horizon is, the less accurate the information is. Nevertheless, these release numbers need to be used to project long-range requirements for materials and labor.

LONG LEAD-TIME ITEMS

Since suppliers are expected to procure raw materials in advance of the customer's actual release authorization to ship, suppliers must write contracts with customers that include the raw materials that need to be purchased in good faith to the customers' forecasts. Suppliers need to be compensated for procuring materials that are not consumed due to reductions in the customer requirements within the agreed upon lead time.

In order for suppliers to protect themselves from obsolescence, the supplier's computer system must be able to generate high fabrication and high raw material numbers based on the customers' highest numbers released. The generation of the high raw and high fabrication numbers allows suppliers to monitor customer demand from the original planned output to another level of planned production. If a customer has increased the demand beyond the original balance-out number, the supplier must contact the customer and discuss the consequences of the increases. In some cases, there are no additional costs. In other cases, there is a cost to have a supplier set up for a short run of materials and to procure more products if necessary.

The high fabrication release is the authorization for the supplier to make and hold completed product; high raw material release is the authorization for the supplier to purchase raw materials. In any balance-out situation, customers would be obligated to purchase the high-fabrication and high-raw-materials amounts they sent to suppliers in the form of releases. Since the dollar impact can be a major issue on balancing-out components, a more detailed discussion is offered in Chapter 20.

MANAGING CUSTOMER CHANGES

Customers are sometimes slow to send releases to suppliers when there is a new product or a pending change that modifies the component composition. If a customer has not sent releases to the plant, a planner must enter releases into MRP manually in order to generate component releases. In reality, the plant is protecting itself from a potential shortage by entering in releases for the customer when the customer does not generate them effectively. These releases are generally called "firm" releases, meaning the suppliers' notice to ship or the suppliers' notice to build and hold. Firm releases are MRP generated based on a firmed-up window of time for supplier releases, manually placed into the system by a planner in order to generate supplier releases, or generated by customers to suppliers as shipping authorizations.

Firm releases are never modified by the MRP system, even when customer demand falls off or is canceled, so care must be taken when planners use firm releases for plant scheduling. When the demand for a component part changes, planners must manually modify or delete the firm release.

Firm releases are also used for shipping authorization for the supply base. A firm release notifies suppliers to ship materials to the customer.

Suppliers generally hold requesting plants responsible for the firm quantity released and do not allow the quantity to be reduced or canceled without some penalty. Therefore, to maintain a low inventory and to have optimum flexibility, it is necessary to limit the number of firm days or weeks of component releases to the supply base.

If firm releases are issued beyond the transit time and are left unmanaged, there will be a potential for either an overstock situation or a shortage. The number of firm days should be carefully considered; the plant needs optimum flexibility to adjust the on-order quantity while allowing the supplier to ship on time.

Since so many companies are now purchasing product from overseas, the firm order period is exceptionally long and does not fit well with the best-in-class release scenarios. The bottom line is that the plant is at risk ordering components with a firm release schedule that far exceeds its customers' firm order period.

INTERNATIONAL RELEASES

Corporations that aspire to save money by sourcing to foreign countries need to understand the risks of incurring obsolescence if customers change order specifications. In negotiating the piece price, plants should inform customers when component sourcing is outside of the United States. If customers accept that the piece price they are receiving is based on a reduced cost due to foreign production, the plant is protected from long lead-time obsolescence issues.

If a customer makes changes to releases in the transit window, then the international supplier may receive a change in release demand within the shipping period that is impossible to meet without incurring an extra cost. International suppliers must make it clear to their customers that releases cannot be changed within the transit window unless customers are willing to pay the additional costs of shipping with an alternate method.

With international supplier purchases, when it is determined that transit time and/or inventory accuracy or that the supplier is not reliable, the only option to protect against plant shortages is to carry more inventory. Although international purchasing contracts may be cost effective, just one premium air shipment can counteract any cost savings in reduced piece prices.

Quality issues with overseas supplies can also contribute to unforeseen expenses. Corporations must evaluate the risk of doing business with a concern that is located in a foreign country. Safety stock must be added to items that may have quality risks.

SUPPLIER LEAD TIME

The MRP system generates planned orders based on gross requirements for the top-level products. Planned orders are moved, increased, and decreased by the inventory computer system so that no maintenance is required other than ensuring that the plant's computer system is correctly interpreting customers' releases. Planned orders are used to project requirements in the future, and suppliers should not ship to them. Suppliers should use planned orders to forecast component requirements from their suppliers and to manage labor in their plant.

A new product may not always have an established start-up lead time before the supplier can use just the transit time to order components. Lead time for new products may include the time it takes to purchase new equipment, build dies, purchase raw materials, and manufacture the start-up product. Once the supplier begins making product to a schedule, then the lead time should become the transit time.

Today's marketplace frowns on suppliers that maintain a lead time greater than the transit time. Any supplier that quotes a lead time greater than transit time has a process that is not stable enough to produce product on demand or is maintaining a zero inventory at the purchaser's expense. Suppliers that can afford to carry zero inventory and demand long lead times from customers most likely produce the only product available.

Purchase order contract negotiators generally fail to include the amount of short-term increase that a plant can order without incurring penalties. There will be times when the plant needs to order components that exceed the firm or planned requirements. Without such a clause in the contract, the plant is in a precarious position when it needs more material in the short term. The supplier can negotiate with the plant on its own terms. The result may be a setup charge, break-in fees, overtime charges, and possible premium freight. Purchase orders should also contain the expected capacity of the supplier in both short and long term.

Another method of guaranteeing product in the short term is to set up an agreement to buy machine time. Buying machine time guarantees that the customer can increase volumes up to the machine time purchased. This method is a good idea when many customers share the same equipment, as it gives the plant the edge when product demand is increased.

INTERNATIONAL LEAD TIMES

There is a direct correlation between the amounts of inventory on hand and the transit times for components. The longer the transit time, the more inventories that must be carried to protect the plant from shortages. International procurements continue to increase in an effort to reduce overall product cost. The disadvantage of international purchases lies in the inability of the ordering plant to maintain a consistent flow of materials without having to carry large inventories.

As foreign manufacturers increase their market share, they may establish warehouses in the United States to alleviate the pressures of scheduling international requirements.

There is a careful balance between lowering inventory and freight expenses. Reducing inventory by increasing the frequency of shipments can result in unacceptable freight expenses. Plant managers and controllers need to ensure that the cost of lowering the inventory does not lead to increased freight expenses. Well-planned and managed releases will accomplish the objective of lowering inventories without a significant increase in freight expenses, provided production does not fall behind schedule.

TRANSIT TIME VERSUS FREIGHT COSTS

Companies pursuing the lowest inventories need to exercise care when selecting the modes of transportation. Full truckloads of materials are generally less expensive to transport than daily shipments by less-than-truckload (LTL) carriers; therefore, a careful evaluation of freight costs versus inventory costs is required.

Establishing milk runs—having a full truck carrier pick up components for the plant at several supplier locations—combining loads with sister plants, and using the correct LTL carriers that service a particular region can help reduce costs and lower the inventories.

Some major companies have created pool points to which suppliers are authorized to ship. Pool points are effective where enough freight can be gathered for a full-truckload carrier to deliver to the plant. This process is often referred to as cross-docking.

LOWER LEAD-TIME INHIBITERS

Companies often make the mistake of eliminating the corporate traffic function. In today's complex purchasing environment, expertise in logistics management is required to keep the cost of transportation to a minimum. The corporate traffic function can maintain the lowest possible transportation costs throughout the corporation and can write major agreements with carriers to cover multiple plant locations.

Some companies fail to consider the piece price cost reduction efforts that purchasing is tasked with versus the transportation costs that result from the supply decision that reduces the piece price but increases the transportation costs. True piece price reductions are those that take freight costs into consideration.

Some companies have moved the corporate traffic function into the plants, aiming to increase the plant's motivation for reducing freight expenses; however, by making this move, companies lose global efforts of reducing freight. Companies with several plants within the same general region will lose the benefit of reducing freight expenses by combining shipments and the advantage that comes with negotiating corporate contracts.

The only viable alternative to a corporate transportation manager is to contract with a third-party logistics firm that will manage all of the corporation's transportation efforts. Companies should perform a detailed cost benefit analysis to determine if they should use the total services of a logistics company, manage the freight internally, or use a combination of both.

A plant's internal lead time should always be zero. Adding any lead time to any level in the bill of materials will compound the inventory value by the number of days added to the total process. Lead time should exist only at the component level, and this lead time should equate only to the transit time, as described.

In a continuous process, there is no value in adding lead time in MRP for finished goods. Companies must use lead-time parameters carefully in order to maintain their inventory goals.

Finished good levels should be managed by having enough products available for the customer on the day that the customer wants the products shipped. For example, if a manufacturing process is capable of 100 pieces per hour, then the minimum balance number should be set at 100 times the number of hours/days needed to produce the required shipment quantity, to the customer's schedules, on time, plus some safety stock to allow for short-term increases. This calculation becomes complex when customers require shipments on different days of the week that are not separated by the same length of time.

Some supplier releases are driven by the particular day of the week because of shipping arrangements. In this case, materials and production departments must have the capability to build inventory to the ship day. The calculation for the minimum balance becomes more complicated, but not impossible, with the need to ship to the customer on an odd schedule, such as every Tuesday and Friday.

The method of using a minimum balance calculated by MRP for finished goods is unreliable when a ship day is imposed since this method is calculated by adding the demand over a specified number of days, dividing this number by the number of days in the demand period, and then multiplying the result by the number of days desired to be on hand. It is better for the materials department to input the calculation in order to ensure that finished goods will be available when they need to be shipped.

The MRP calculation method is unreliable when:

- Demand fluctuates
- Demand is inconsistent or lumpy
- There is no demand for a period since the average for the period may actually be lower than the normal customer daily delivery quantity

MRP minimum and maximum calculations are especially vulnerable in November, when December demand is usually 50 percent of the norm due to holidays. Plants can be caught off guard and short inventory in January when customers' schedules pick up.

Materials planners must carefully monitor the releases in down periods to prevent shortages caused by lowered minimum computer calculations.

Most companies are managing finished goods levels with a visual system of management. The visual system, which is simply a count of the finished goods at the beginning of the shift and then a comparison of the current inventory to the customer's next release quantity, is the best management system, since it is real time and does not depend on someone creating a production schedule. Since production schedules are usually generated from spreadsheets, there is the possibility of errors. Spreadsheet information is outdated the moment it is printed because operations are continuous. Data may be missing from a spreadsheet because of finished goods that have not been entered into MRP. The visual system is the best system of replenishment because it means that product levels are the responsibility of department managers, who need to keep up to date with customer release schedules.

CHAPTER 7

INVENTORY ACCURACY

What are the signs that inventory inaccuracy is an issue in a plant? Inventory inaccuracy may cause excessive downtime in a plant due to lack of materials.

Many companies schedule monthly physical inventories because they do not trust the perpetual numbers. These physical inventories are a waste of company time and money and prove that no one understands how to manage materials.

Numerous factors can directly influence the inventory accuracy. The most important practice that a materials team can adopt is developing verification systems to ensure that all data in and out of the materials requirement planning (MRP) system is correct. Although double-checking takes time, it is worth the effort to keep the inventory as accurate as possible.

Inventory inaccuracy may result from software issues, data input/output errors, transaction errors, cycle-count errors, and unreported scrap.

The software maker or the company's information systems department should resolve software issues that create problems with inventory management. Most software issues occur with the transfer of data from one software package to another or in daily updates where numerous programs interface with each other and one has crashed. An overloaded hardware system is usually the root cause of system crashes.

If a plant and/or company is plagued with constant shortages due to incorrect perpetual inventories on the computer system, there needs to be an extensive review of how the inventory is managed. The number-one cause of firefighting is the inability to control the computer system inventory (perpetual).

Once people lose faith in the accuracy of the data in the computer system, they usually establish methods to circumvent the system, such as using expediters and stock chasers.

Many planners revert to managing the inventory with spreadsheets. The danger with using spreadsheets is the fact that they could contain errors that allow the generation of inaccurate releases.

MANAGING THE COMPUTER-CONTROLLED INVENTORY SYSTEM

Efforts to correct the inventory on the system may be in vain due to a host of reasons, both within and beyond the control of the materials group. Even when a new perpetual inventory is posted to the system from a physical inventory, if the reasons for the inaccuracies are not corrected, the information quickly becomes inaccurate.

The problem of maintaining an accurate perpetual inventory can be compounded by efforts to correct the system with arbitrary inventory adjustments. Compounding errors result from failure to identify the root causes for the inventory inaccuracy and take corrective action. However, due to time pressure and inability to understand the root causes, quick adjustments may be the materials group's only way to adjust the inventory.

The lack of time to research the root causes stems from having an overwhelming number of cycle-count adjustments and not enough people to manage the situation.

Errors can be compounded by inaccurately correcting a problem that is corrected later by the proper transaction, such as by finally entering a missing receipt into the system. Entering the missing receipt actually doubles the amount of the inventory when a cycle count was used earlier to correct the system.

Errors are compounded when one cycle count reduces the inventory and the next cycle count increases it. Such changes render the inventory extremely inaccurate without a double-check verification.

Inventory inaccuracy is a symptom of system failures, lack of discipline, and lack of knowledge to implement proper system controls. If an overwhelming number of cycle-count adjustments are made monthly, the materials group generally is in an endless firefighting mode. A concerted effort is required to get back to the basics. One aim of this book is to provide the insight required for putting out the fires.

Inventory accuracy depends on the plant's ability to control receiving accuracy, proper storage, scrap reporting, rework, vendor count, bills of materials, cycle counting, shipping accuracy, finished product reporting, and data input/output control.

With so many direct inputs into the system that can affect inventory accuracy, it is difficult to ensure that all transactions are correct. Any system that relies on human input is bound to contain errors. Those who understand how to minimize the errors will have the advantage.

If inventory control was on par with accounting practices, perhaps the view of controlling materials in the plant would change. Accountants are simply not allowed to adjust the ledger in order to balance the month. Accountants also have double-check systems that allow them to reconcile the ledger. Why should inventory control be any different from controlling the company's cash? After all, inventory is money.

The level of inventory accuracy usually depends on the plant's ability to formulate corrective action plans from a root cause analysis of a problem. If no corrective action plan is formulated to resolve accuracy issues, the inventory inaccuracy problem continues to compound to a point where every physical inventory results in an unacceptable loss.

Even when the physical inventory does balance within reason in dollars, a part number review may reveal a different result. This may happen when the counts for the highest dollar items in a plant are more accurate than for the rest of the components. For example, if there were

1,000 parts of X, at a cost of $800 each, the inventory would be $800,000. If the balance of 2,500 part numbers totaled $100,000, it would be possible to balance within reason on the ledger during a physical inventory. The materials group's understanding of the dollar structure of the components used would most likely ensure that part X is always correct.

LIMITING ACCESS TO MAKE CHANGES

Too many users with access to make changes in the MRP system are not conducive to good control. The number of people who can affect the perpetual inventory must be limited to those directly responsible for inventory accuracy. No matter how well people are trained, having numerous people enter transactions for finished goods and raw materials will never work effectively.

Inventory control needs to be managed by those who are directly responsible for its accuracy. This philosophy goes against the principles of most top managers, who believe in open and free access to inventory. Open and free access to inventory generally invites people to take what they need. Engineers, service people, and others may fail to inform materials control when they remove inventory.

INVENTORY ACCURACY INFLUENCERS

In some plants, materials department faces a major challenge in convincing the operations department that certain practices are having a negative impact on the perpetual inventory. The major concern for manufacturing is that there is a constant unbroken supply of materials; some of the practices manufacturing employs may actually contribute to the problem.

Excessive work in process is never an advantage to controlling materials, even though it may make sense in order to maintain manufacturing efficiencies. Component parts used in many applications may be used excessively in one product subassembly, thereby artificially creating a shortage for another subassembly process that requires the same component.

Rejected materials and rework is another disadvantage for maintaining inventory accuracy, especially when such materials are allowed to pile up.

Most plants have no formal policy for reporting and reducing inventory that is used in subassemblies that must be reworked or reviewed for disposition. Inventory records will show inventory on hand as available until the subassembly is either used or reported as consumed or scrapped.

A detailed investigation may be required to determine if the scrap reporting, rework, and production reporting systems are contributing to the inventory inaccuracies. The more complex the subassembly to be reworked is, the more difficult it is to capture the correct materials scrapped or used as replacements. Some subassemblies are so complex that it is difficult to determine what components were scrapped. When the component being reworked is very complex, routine cycle-count adjustments need to be made or the whole part needs to be scrapped off the system with any salvageable components placed back on to the system.

The accuracy of reporting scrap is a particular area of concern for materials control. Operations people may be reluctant to assist in improving scrap reporting, since such improvements ultimately may increase the scrap dollars the plant is reporting.

A change of philosophy may be required to improve scrap reporting. Since cycle-count losses generally are attributed to ineffective scrap reporting systems, combining cycle counts and scrap reporting systems into a total scrap number may benefit the plant scrap reduction management effort. Combining these amounts leads to a common plant focus on reducing the loss of inventory. Top management needs to decide if inventory accuracy and true scrap reporting will benefit the bottom line.

Increased inventory accuracy from accurate scrap reporting will reduce expedited freight expenses and lead to increased productivity due to an unbroken supply of materials.

Inventory begins with the receipt of components and raw materials from suppliers. Are the suppliers accurate in the counts they are packing and shipping? The answer is a resounding yes. Although suppliers are not in the business of shorting materials to customers, errors can happen. Repeated shortages for a particular component may be cause to verify the supplier's package count. Some suppliers use counters to load box counts; there may be an issue with the counter itself or the weighing scale may be out of calibration.

Counting components received may be a difficult task due to the nature of the product. Plants need to purchase the correct equipment to verify the counts. Small lightweight parts need small counting scales. Larger bulky materials may need a floor scale that can handle heavy materials.

Sometimes the way the items are packaged makes counting the parts in the container difficult. If the packaging can be changed without incurring more costs, it should be changed.

The plant's receiving system must be robust. Every receipt of product must be verified in total to the packing slip. Even if there is a bar code scanning process, product receipt must be verified to the packing slip to ensure that all of the boxes or counts on the packing slip have been received properly.

One measure of a plant's ability to receive properly is reflected in the number of calls from suppliers claiming lack of payment for items shipped.

The number of supplier invoices that are not paid may reveal that the packing slips are being interpreted incorrectly or are missed entirely. Inaccurate data entry is the leading cause of nonpayments to suppliers. This situation can be rectified by implementing a simple double-check process at the end of every day. Printing a receiving report from MRP and then verifying the accuracy of the entries is a simple process that will save countless hours looking for the error.

A good practice is to scan receipts into the MRP system, but this is not the perfect system. The scanning process prevents the human data entry errors; however, it creates another problem: The people who scan the bar codes often fail to scan some of the boxes or skids of materials. It is essential for the receiving department to double-check the entries into the system by comparing the packing slip totals to the scanned totals.

It is not difficult to understand why product gets to the manufacturing floor without being received properly. One reason may be that materials are needed immediately, and those who need them to continue operations usually take the products, bypassing receiving. Evidence of this action is the finding of packing slips still taped on boxes located on the production floor.

No matter how much training people undergo about the importance of receiving, it easy for someone to take materials and forget about receiving them into the system. The answer to this issue is not locking the receiving area; some people believe bolt cutters were made for this problem. The answer is to finish the job of receiving on a daily basis, leaving nothing to chance.

When packing slips are missing, temporary receivers must be issued so that the materials are entered into the system. Every temporary receiver needs to be replaced by the original without the original inadvertently being entered into the system.

What about actually losing parts in the plant? There is nothing worse than shutting down a process in the plant for lack of a part that is physically available. Everyone in materials control understands that this does happen. The thought process of everything has a place is a good practice to follow; however, occasionally materials are placed in the wrong location. This situation may be difficult to resolve, since the only way the misplaced materials are discovered is when someone needs a component from that particular location. Misplacing materials can be attributed to carelessness. It can cost the company in downtime hours or expedited freight to the customer. Product always needs to be placed in locations were it can easily be retrieved.

Some suppliers can add a location on the package label. However, this system is difficult to maintain when product storage locations are changed often. Nissan Corporation requires that all suppliers print the storage location on their product labels. Suppliers are responsible for ensuring that the label locations are current, and a penalty is imposed for incorrect location designations. An alternative to this system is to print the identification label with the storage location upon receiving the components into the system.

Some plants have tried to control the physical location of components as they move from one location to another by entering the change in locations in the computer system. This system is rarely successful, since it is time consuming, and people often forget to enter the change or do so inaccurately. Using rack locations in the computer system generates negative balances when transfers are incorrect.

The problem of negatives from lack of transfers or incorrect keying can be devastating to the perpetual inventory and the ordering process. Depending on the reorder system, additional supply releases may be generated for negative inventories that show in the computer locations.

The best practice to store materials is to use the inspection label to identify where to place materials and eliminate the need for storage locations in the system. This practice will also ensure that the inspection label is present, since it contains the storage location.

The most prevalent inventory control issue is lack of proper scrap control. Lack of scrap reporting can have a devastating effect on the inventory accuracy. How can we control this monster? One way to see if this is a concern is to tour the plant and look at where the scrap is being placed and how it is being processed. Fear of discipline from management may cause employees to push aside or hide scrap. Employees who create scrap by using incorrect processing methods or mishandling materials need to be reprimanded even if management believes that this will have adverse consequences on scrap reporting accuracy.

One alternative is to place bins designated for scrap in highly visible areas in the plant nearest to the operation. The bins should be clearly marked as such. All opportunities to hide or throw scrap away should be removed from the manufacturing floor. Trash barrels should be open containers used only for paper waste. Open containers discourage people from dumping rejected materials into them. For larger, more complex parts, the scrap bin may have to be located away from the workstation. In this case, line out on the floor exactly where the scrap bin is to be located and instruct people to use only this bin for that particular scrap item. Except for a designated few people who have no direct production responsibility, workers should never have direct access to trash compactors or outside trash bins.

Proper training can address the issues of poor housekeeping and allowing people the opportunity to push aside bad material. Acknowledging that everything needs to be in an assigned place is a start to good housekeeping. Lining out designated spots on the floor, wall, racks, and bins, and then labeling the spots will help keep the work areas organized.

Plants with hundreds of employees occasionally have to deal with disgruntled employees who attempt sabotage by trashing. Access to trash compactors should be carefully monitored and managed.

Raising the visibility of scrap on the floor will be a winning situation for the company and the employees. Employees should be encouraged to help resolve the issues that generate scrap by being a part of the improvement process.

Any plant that has a scrap reporting issue should respond appropriately to raise the visibility of the problem with the manufacturing people. One method that works is to hold all scrap right where it is created. That scrap should not be removed until the plant manager, materials manager, engineering manager, and the controller walk through and sign off for the disposal. In this way, the plant manager becomes aware of the issues that generate the scrap, the materials manager has the count for inventory accuracy, the controller has the dollar impact, and the supervisor and employees will be more alert about enforcing proper processes. The engineering manager may be able to correct the situation with some equipment or component modifications. The walk-through should continue until the processes are under control at every workstation.

Everyone needs to be informed that scrap affects the supply of material that keeps the process running. It is also important to remove the pressures of scrap dollars and percentages from the floor and replace them with proactive thoughts on how to improve the process.

Once scrap is controlled, the next step is to understand how it can be reported in the system. Scrap items at the component level with no added value are easily recorded. The recording challenge is when an item destined for the scrap bin contains a number of components. The process of recording scrap for every small component can be complex, time consuming, and perhaps not efficient or even effective. The best practice is to design a process sheet with a phantom level— a level in the bill of materials that is always zero and is bypassed by MRP—that contains the operations accounting for every component added to the finished product at the workstation. Scrapping at the correct operation level will reduce the components correctly in the system.

Reworking product by replacing a portion of the assembly creates a different reporting issue. Not only is there scrap, but there are parts used for replacement. Development of a rework reporting process that reports the additional component usage and scrap can be accomplished with some thought. Depending on the complexity of the product and the number of components in the rework product, the process of reporting the components scrapped and used can be easy or difficult.

Keeping the inventory accurate on the computer system is time consuming, challenging, and sometimes difficult; however, it can be accomplished. The first step is to list the possible issues that may cause inventory discrepancies.

Some possible categories for inventory inaccuracies are receiving mistakes, shipping errors, unreported scrap, bill of material errors, and production reporting errors. Determining the root cause of an inventory loss takes time; when the root cause is determined, appropriate actions must be taken to prevent the problem from continuing.

The other area that influences inventory accuracy is the accuracy of the bill of materials. Errors may be caused when a change is made to the product but the person responsible for the bill-of-materials generation is not notified. Often the original bill of materials drafted by engineering is used, but materials may have changed since the original product design. Too many bills of materials are entered from paper documentation without actual site or piece verification. The engineering department should verify every bill of materials with every change. The best practice is to review the bill of materials by physically observing the process at the site of manufacture.

Whether products are scanned into the computer system or not, the entries of finished goods into the system must be verified and a process of error detection and correction must be implemented. Inaccurate finished goods are generally due to missed scans into stores or the reworking of product.

When product is removed from the storeroom for repacking, that inventory must be taken out of the system and placed into the system as the product is placed back into stores. This process avoids potential errors of entering reworked finished goods as new product. The company's controller must always sign off on the reversing method; some MRP systems cannot change the labor absorption that has been used and the controller will need to manually adjust the labor costs on the ledger correctly.

Another issue that can influence inventory accuracy is the way in which returns to suppliers are managed. Materials that have been placed on hold by the plant may sit around for a while, awaiting an agreement to return the parts to the supplier. If the inventory management process does not compensate for parts that are unusable, the inventory is overstated and there is a chance for a shortage. For this reason, it is important to establish a specific location in which to place rejected materials. The inventory in this location is counted in the physical inventory but it is not available as usable for the reordering process.

The more accurate the inventory is, the more efficient the plant will be and fewer inventories will be required to support the process. Exhibit 7.1 summarizes the most prevalent inventory influencers.

EXHIBIT 7.1   *Major Inventory Accuracy Influencers*

Scrap reporting

Bill of materials

Production reporting errors

Cycle counting

Unreported alternate usage

Shipping issues

Receiving errors

CHAPTER 8

CYCLE COUNTING

If implemented properly and managed effectively, cycle counting will minimize premium freight and contribute substantially to uptime in the plant. If a company is faced with shortages while the perpetual inventory is still showing a balance, issues with the cycle-counting process need to be identified and resolved. There may be so many issues with the perpetual inventory that cycle counting alone cannot fix the problems. Cycle counting is employed when input and output information is incorrect or missing.

Cycle counting should reveal issues that need to be corrected. It is important to address the issues uncovered by a good cycle-counting process and not just make adjustments to the system without an investigation.

CONVINCING ARGUMENT FOR CYCLE COUNTING

If a plant is not cycle counting despite a strong need to do so, the challenge will be to convince top management of the need to add additional people to manage the process. To do so, set up a pilot cycle-counting program for components that are frequently out of balance in the perpetual inventory and that have contributed to plant downtime. List each imbalance, and implement a corrective action that resolves the shortage issue. Maintain a chart of the progress made with identifying and resolving issues. Providing top management with positive results that show cost avoidance should be convincing enough to get the cycle-counting program started.

When the physical inventory balances to ledger with dollars, top managers are reluctant to add labor for a cycle-count program. Yet total dollars of inventory versus a physical inventory that closely balances in total dollars does not mean that the inventory is accurate on a part-by-part basis, especially when there are many small-dollar, high-volume components and a few large-dollar items. As mentioned elsewhere, materials people will keep the higher-value items correct because they know what the impact is.

A good cycle-counting program begins with identifying what parts need to be counted and on what frequency. The best place to start is with those parts that have been adjusted frequently or have a high frequency of loss. The complexity and length of time to perform cycle counts depends on the degree of precision required. It may be necessary to scale-count all parts in order to accomplish the plant's required cycle-count level. It may be necessary to hand-count parts in order to obtain a good count.

COMPUTER-GENERATED CYCLE COUNTS

Often a cycle-count program built into the materials requirement planning (MRP) program can be utilized. Computer-generated programs are designed to select items randomly and then keep the selection process going based on the ABC[1] criteria developed in the system. Although such systems seemingly will work to provide the counts required daily, they are not recommended when there is a high rate of shortages or gains of various components on a daily basis. If stock-outs are an issue, it is a better practice to manually select those items that are responsible for downtime first, investigate the root causes, and then take corrective action no matter what the value is.

The computer-generated list of cycle counting using the ABC process should be reserved for those inventories that have a 95 percent or higher accuracy rate.

An inventory accuracy calculation is needed to determine where the plant is in comparison to accuracy level expectations. The inventory accuracy rate can be calculated in many ways. Some methods can skew the numbers such that it looks like there are no problems. A recommendation for calculating inventory accuracy is presented at the end of this chapter, but it is not the only true method.

In order to use the computer-generated cycle-count program, all parts need to be labeled or categorized in levels of importance. The process that is generally accepted is assigning the ABC levels of control. The A items are counted more frequently than the B items; C items are counted even less frequently than the A and B items. The A items are generally those that have the highest dollar usage and are the most expensive parts. However, an A item can be a component that has a high risk of inventory loss, such as a small washer. The B items can be classified as those of medium value. C items are generally those that are least expensive and least likely for count loss. Note that a C item that has a high volume and is a chronic problem should be classified as an A item until the shrinkage issues are resolved.

As a rule, A items should be counted weekly, B items biweekly, and C items monthly. Once a cycle-count pattern is established for each component, the ABC classification of the part may need to be changed from one level to the next. ABC classifications initially should be determined on cost and usage, but the planners' subjective view is the real governing factor.

CYCLE-COUNTING PROFICIENCY

A robust and accurate cycle-counting program is depends on the selection of who will be responsible for the counting. Cycle counting can be extremely complicated, especially when the component to be counted is located in several areas of the plant or it is contained in work-in-process (WIP) inventories. Cycle counters must know where any particular part may be located. In addition, they must be able to estimate the quantity of small parts in open boxes and to find all of the locations in the plant where the component is used. Most materials professionals would agree that estimation of small components is acceptable when the box on the assembly line is open. Complicating the counting process by scale counting (weighing) washers or screws may not contribute to any significant inventory accuracy. If estimation can provide acceptable results, then that should be the best practice.

The success of a cycle counter can be measured by the number of fluctuating adjustments in the system. There is reason for scrutiny when a downward adjustment is countered by an upward adjustment in the next cycle count. Vacillating inventory adjustments are a sign that the inventory is difficult to count or that the methods being used are insufficient. Perhaps the cycle counter does not fully understand how to establish the timing of when to count or simply is not fit for the job.

CYCLE-COUNTING CRITERIA

Timing is crucial in order to obtain a good cycle count. First, there needs to be an inventory of the finished goods to ensure that there are no reporting issues. If the inventory of finished goods varies often, then cycle-counting components should no t be started until the control issues are corrected for finished goods. Keep in mind that the finished goods reported and entered into the system back-flush[2] the component inventory. Prior to a components cycle count, there needs to be verification that all of the finished goods have been reported in the system for those items that are to be counted. In addition, there needs to be a count of finished goods that are in partial packages along with any finished goods that may be on hold or undergoing repair.

Counting components where there is a multitude of operations or WIP may complicate the cycle-counting process, but it is not impossible. If there is a minimal amount of WIP, as there should be, it may be determined that the inventory in these parts can be bypassed because the value or the volume of the component being counted is of little significance to the overall count. As stated, some parts may be estimated.

How precise the count needs to be depends on the nature of the product, the volumes of part used, and the cost of the components. It does not make sense to count with precision components that are inexpensive or high-volume parts that are prone to some shrinkage due to the nature of the process. Using a process of estimation for open boxes of components will usually suffice in obtaining a good overall count. Candidates for estimation are generally screws, washers, liquids, and other small inexpensive components that have large inventories on hand.

The cycle-counting process can be complex if the component being counted is located all over the plant. Generally, parts that are used in many areas of the plant are small and inexpensive. It may not make sense to count all of the inexpensive high-volume parts. It is actually the best practice to keep more of these components on hand and count the unopened boxes. For example, if a washer has a cost of .015, having even 100,000 of them on hand equates to only $1,500. Using a refined count for a part like this one is a waste of effort and time.

Note: When the plant determines that a three-day inventory is the goal, materials people need to understand the impact of the smallest-dollar items on the total value of the inventory. A three-day supply of washers may be 10,000 washers, or $150. Trying to maintain a three-day supply of this part may not be the best practice, especially if the total inventory is in the millions. The better practice is to carry the 100,000 washers on hand.

It is necessary to ensure that the components being counted are not in receiving waiting to be delivered to the assembly location or in a quality hold location. As previously discussed, the computer system should indicate a quality hold location.

Whether it is a penny or $50, the costs of air freight and downtime need to be avoided. The cost of the part alone should never be the deciding factor as to when a component should be counted. Selection of the components to be counted at the appropriate time is most important to ensure that there is a minimal chance of a shortage occurrence.

There are a number of reasons why counts do not match the system. A tracking form needs to be developed to identify the root cause of the adjustment. Since a cycle-count adjustment may not be avoidable, it may be necessary to establish a percentage of adjustment that can be made without a formal investigation. Attempting to determine the reason for every cycle-count adjustment may prove to be too cumbersome and may result in a reduction in counts or adjustments as time permits.

The cycle-count form should contain check boxes for the reason that an adjustment is required. Avoiding the use of "other" or "unknown" as a category will force the counter to determine the reason for the adjustment. However, after some time has elapsed, there may not be a reasonable explanation and the root of the problem may never be determined.

The cycle-count form may or may not require a signature from a higher level of authority in the company. The recommendation is to set a percentage limit on changes that can be made by the cycle counter without a manager's signature. There may be a need to include dollars as a limiting factor, depending on the value of a unit. The controller needs to be in the loop; he or she should be the top person to sign off on a cycle count, since the month-end numbers are going to reflect the loss or gain in inventory dollars.

Cycle-count losses can be attributed to a number of factors. The most prevalent issue for an inventory adjustment is loss due to scrap. Many small components that are subject to shrink in the every day manufacturing process are difficult to capture in the scrap reporting process. Reworking a part of an assembly by replacing rejected components is another issue that may not be controlled properly, leading to a cycle-count adjustment. Cycle-count adjustments may be the result of inaccurate bills of materials or the result of a system glitch that prevents the system from recording usage properly.

Gains usually come from components that were received without being entered them into the system. It is important not to arbitrarily adjust the system without a full investigation of why there are more components on hand than shown in the system. The best way to resolve this issue is to contact the supplier, compare the shipping and receiving dates and quantities, and then compare the cumulative balances of the supplier versus the plant. Any increase that is not attributed to a lost supplier packing slip needs to be held in abeyance and recounted to ensure that the cycle count taken was correct. It is to be hoped that the cycle-count increase was not due to an earlier cycle-count decrease.

Generally, no increase adjustment to the system should be allowed until it is absolutely verified that the potential adjustment was caused from a previous cycle-count error, a bill of material error, or a physical inventory mistake.

Developing a list of reasons for cycle-count adjustments depends on the nature of the business. It is best to start with a few known problems and then modify the listing as new issues appear. Some of the reasons for cycle-count variances are receiving errors, bill of material error, production reporting error, quality hold previous cycle count error, scrap issue, supplier count error, physical inventory error, and computer system error due to fall out or corrupt files.

Incorrect bills of materials are always high on the error list. In order to purchase components, bills of materials need to be entered into the system prior to the actual production start date. Issues may arise when the actual production begins if changes have been made to the product that has not been conveyed properly to the people responsible for maintaining the bills of materials. One method of minimizing the bill errors is to set up a check system to finalize the bill when actual production begins. The review of the bill of materials can be as simple as visually observing the production process and verifying the usage or acquiring a finished product and verifying the components actually used compared to the bill in a controlled location. In any event, a failure to verify the bill of materials can be a costly mistake for the plant.

Certain components seem to disappear from production floors. A closer look at why parts seem to disappear may reveal that parts are placed on hold and then moved to a hold location or even returned to the supplier without the proper recording transaction in MRP. The plant process for handling quality hold items needs to support the planning process by insuring the materials are processes timely and accurately.

There needs to be a process for reporting the inventory accuracy in a plant. Accuracy must be reported very carefully. Some methods of displaying cycle-count accuracy are little more than graphs showing the percentage of accuracy based on the adjustment percentage. A percent of adjustment is not an accurate method of reporting. The percentage number of 95 percent inventory accuracy based on total numbers counted versus net adjustments is meaningless except to show that everything looks good.

The best practice is to measure the cycle-count accuracy from a *baseline* count. The adjustment percentage from one cycle date to the next is the true measure of inventory accuracy on a part-by-part basis. The best practice is to establish a baseline count for each part number counted and then record the date counted and the adjustment made. The next time the part number is counted, record the date and the adjustment made. Count the number of days past from the base cycle count. Take the adjustment quantity and then divide it by the number of days past. The result of this calculation is the true shrink or gain on a daily basis, and it is a measure of the true inventory accuracy.

For example, part ABC was counted 30 days ago. The adjustment quantity today is 120 pieces. The loss is 4 pieces per day. This number has a lot more meaning to the cost of the process than a percentage number. In dollars, the loss may be $2.00 per day. Perhaps it is $10.00 per day. In that case, the reason for the loss of this part should be determined.

It is hoped that there is no pilferage or intentional disposal of components in the plant. It is important to make it difficult for people to cause line downtime or profit losses due to improper actions. Scrap bins, trash compactors, and other disposal areas should be placed properly and their use monitored, and accessibility should be limited.

NOTES

1. "A" items are materials that are of the highest value. "B" items are materials that are deemed to be of significant cost but less than "A"

items. "C" items are materials of the lowest value. The finance department is generally responsible for assigning the ABC designations based on total dollars carried in the inventory.

2. Back-flushing is the process of relieving the inventory of component items by entering the finished product into the MRP system. The bill of materials is searched and the parts are reduced from the inventory according to the usage times the number of finished goods reported.

CHAPTER 9

RELEASES TO SUPPLIERS

M ost materials requirement planning (MRP) systems are set up to receive customer releases through electronic data interchange (EDI). Then the received EDI drives the component releases directly by exploding down through the bill of materials to the component levels. This system works well except when the customer does not stabilize the releases or the information in the MRP system changes dramatically because of internal data input/output issues.

As mentioned earlier, most customers, especially original equipment manufacturers, produce at a consistent rate unless a manufacturing issue or some other issue prevents them from making their daily rate.

Releases from customers that show an erratic demand are a concern for the supplier, especially when the demand is consistently pushed out into the future as a new week begins. Suppliers generally mistrust releases that vacillate; therefore, suppliers will second-guess the customer's releasing strategy. Second-guessing can lead to disaster when the customer actually requires the scheduled entire product or decides to work extra time to make up for lost production without notification.

If the customer's short-term demand constantly results in the reschedule of material or a cancellation, leaving the supplier with inventory manufactured but not shipped, the customer should be contacted directly to learn why the releases are changing. It is far better to communicate with the customer than to assume that the releases are always overstated.

Perhaps the customer intends to use the products it has on order. An issue with another supplier or a production issue may be keeping the customer from meeting production goals. When the customer resolves the issue, there could be a larger-than-normal pull of materials, which may place the plant in a precarious situation.

MANAGING DEMAND IN THE PLANT

A forecasting or planning module that has the capability of overriding EDI in the MRP system can be used to improve ordering. The system combines with the EDI releases or takes the higher of the two, forecast or EDI release. The forecasting or MRP planning module should be used to plan more material than the customer release is generating if there is a need to build ahead to prepare for vacations, planned machine repairs, or engineering changes, or to establish a consistent run rate in the plant.

There are two basic methods to increase the demand over and above the customer demand:

1. Enter a forecast into MRP.
2. Use firm planned orders[1] at the finished good level.

The best practice is to use the MRP planning module and enter firm planned orders for additional finished good planning. Planning at the top level using firm planned orders is in essence the master schedule. Most companies still use master schedules instead of simply using customer demand to drive releases.

The advantage of using firm planned orders versus a computer forecast is that the firm planned order quantity is automatically reduced when production is reported. The forecast amount is not usually reduced until the planner manually reduces it. The result of using firm planned orders to exceed customer demand is that the additional demand is sent to the suppliers. The suppliers will see the demand the plant is actually anticipating to manufacture, and shortages will be averted when building more than customers demand.

SUPPLIER RELEASE GENERATION

Customer orders that are not sent EDI must be entered into the computer system manually. These orders are generally sent by facsimile or mail. The best practice is to generate gross requirements[2] equal to an EDI transmission by manually entering shipping lines in the computer system. The major issue with entering releases manually is that it takes a lot of commitment and time to manage them. As with all manual entries, the process can be error prone.

The release generation to suppliers for components must consist of firm releases and planning releases. Firm releases are those that authorize the supplier to build and ship in the current week(s). The generally accepted practice is to issue the least amount of firm release days that enables the supplier to ship to the plant on time.

Some suppliers will request a few weeks of firm orders in order to firm their build schedules. Once a release is firm, it is generally accepted practice to allow the supplier to ship, even if plant demand decreases. MRP generates the firm release by a set of rules managed by planning parameters. The planning parameter for the firm release is usually set in days or weeks for each component.

The delivery date or ship date for a particular component is equal to the accumulated lead time in the MRP system from the top of the bill of material to the lowest level. It is important to recognize that lead times established in the system for each level of production are added to generate a total lead time. The system generates releases to suppliers based on the combined lead times from the system through levels in the bill of materials. Having lead times at all of the levels will result in having more inventory on hand than is required to manage the day-to-day business, especially when the lead times combined above the lowest level is not realistic. For this reason, it is generally accepted practice to set the lead times for work in process (WIP) and finished goods to zero.

As previously discussed, the lead time should be the transit time from the supplier only, plus safety time for nonpull items and just the transit time for pull items. If a safety time feature is not available in the MRP system, then a minimum balance can be computed by MRP or entered manually by a planner. The pull levels for components should be determined by the maximum plant output for the day times the transit time plus a safety number. Plants that use a pull system for components need to restrict firm orders to the visual pull/scanned quantities that are released to the supplier. As each part is scanned for replacement, the planned release is automatically converted into a firm release.

Planning releases show the supplier the anticipated demand for the upcoming weeks and months and they are the suppliers' authorization to purchase raw materials. The supplier planning releases should at a minimum meet the lead times required by the supplier to procure raw materials. Planning releases should be an extension of the plant's build expectations for the next several months. Generally, the farther out planning releases are from the current day, the less reliable they are. However, it is important to show some stability in the planning releases in the short term so that supplying plants can use the releases to forecast sales and manpower.

In the releasing scheme for components, the MRP module usually has a provision for a high fabrication and a high raw number. These numbers are important to generate for suppliers in order to ensure a consistent flow of materials. The high fabrication number is the suppliers' authorization to make and hold product. It is not an authorization to ship product; it is an authorization to make assemblies available to ship. The high raw number is the suppliers' authorization to purchase raw materials. It is the amount of raw material that the plant is authorizing the supplier to purchase.

Many companies find themselves with obsolete materials generated from MRP systems where the planner does not manage the planning parameters correctly. It is important for plants to monitor component releases when there is a pending engineering change so that suppliers are not issued high raw and fabrication numbers that may result in excess material charges to the plant. When phasing out components, it is important to remove all planning parameters, such as safety stock, so that MRP-generated activity does not order excess materials.

Suppliers that use lead times that exceed the transit time to the using plant are generally building make to order. Make-to-order suppliers are not following the current accepted practices of just in time. Plant materials management should work with these suppliers to establish programs to eliminate excessive lead time. The exception to this rule should be for components of extremely low volumes, one of a kind, special order, or components with a low shelf life.

Occasionally customers increase demand without notice in the short term, exceeding the last release quantities by a percentage that causes the plant to scramble. This situation generally occurs when the customer changes the run rate or increases production hours without sufficient notice. Good communication with the customer and a heightened awareness of customers' build schedules and changes can help to avert supply issues. When the actual need exceeds the released requirements for a particular week or month, plants often are forced to pay suppliers for additional setup time, run time, and premium freight. The best scenario is when the materials department can produce the documents to prove the problem is the customers' responsibility.

To prepare for the erratic changes in customer demand, the purchasing contract for suppliers should contain a percentage of increase in a period that is allowed without penalty. The customer contract with the plant should contain a provision for large increases that extend beyond the agreed run rate. Plants should pass on to their customers the costs incurred with running overtime, expediting freight, or paying suppliers' setup time and other costs.

Release system parameters must be set correctly in MRP to generate the desired demand to suppliers. Every plant release system should transmit delivery dates or ship dates to suppliers. If the receiving plant is paying for the freight, ship dates are usually generated to the supplier. The supplier is then responsible for shipping the product on the day and time requested. The receiving plant would then need to ensure that the carriers are delivering the product on a timely basis to the plant. If the supplier is paying for the freight, then the plant should issue the due/delivery date. The supplier in this case is responsible for carrier selection and ensuring delivery is attained. The best materials practice is for the plant to generate ship dates to suppliers.

Proper planning parameters in the system are crucial for the timing of deliveries from suppliers. Planning parameters that are incorrectly set in the computer system may lead to supply issues. All computer systems should have entry fields for the transit time and day of shipment. The "day of shipment" is the days of the week that a supplier ships to the plant. The release sent to suppliers will have ship dates that equate to particular days of the week, as specified in the planning module. The day of shipment(s) should be set to a frequency that carefully balances freight expenses with the required quantity to be shipped.

For immediate component shipments, pull systems are widely replacing computer system releases generated from MRP. MRP releases are generally regarded as planned releases only, with no firm commitment until a pull signal is generated.

The simplest form of a pull system is to send a daily spreadsheet of part numbers and quantities to a supplier that need to be shipped to the plant. The drawback to this system is when the supplier is not able to or fails to retrieve the releases from the facsimile machine.

A better ordering system uses scanning equipment to scan material that is taken directly to the line and opened. The scan of the material becomes a supplier release via the MRP system and EDI generation.

The next generation of supply management is though supplier-managed inventory. Through this process, the supplier reads the inventory on hand in a plant on the Web and sends materials based on a min/max (minimum/maximum) system. In order for this system to be effective, the perpetual inventory in a facility needs to be exact. Any plant that has not resolved its inventory accuracy issues, WIP control issues, and last-minute production overtime plans will fail with this system.

SHORTAGE CONTROL

Shortage control is the process of ensuring that components are received on time into the plant and then delivered to the manufacturing floor before the assembly process is affected.

As easy as it sounds, shortages are the biggest issue for material control and the plant. Avoiding shortages in a plant is the most difficult and challenging task that faces materials control. The sheer number of contributing factors that can cause a shortage is why managing inventory without a shortage arising is so difficult.

The best process to corralling the shortage issue is to develop methods that alert the materials department of potential shortages. The best practices involve systems of visual management, which are discussed in Chapter 19.

Using the materials requirement planning system or via the MRP system with fixed minimums by the materials group, a report can be generated to list the inventory items below the minimum balance. All items on the "minimum balance" report are verified with a cycle count to ensure that the MRP system inventory is correct. The materials department uses judgment to determine if there is a need to contact the supplier for a status from the current releases. The drawback to generating the minimum report is not managing the "fixed" inventory minimum balances correctly on a routine basis.

Another method is to review a past-due supplier release report. The MRP system generates this report by searching through all records containing release date information to suppliers, then extracting all supplier line items that show past due. The materials department then reviews each item on the list to ensure that it has been shipped or planned to ship to the plant before there is a shortage issue. The major issue with this report is that some items listed may have a shortfall in the plant before the review is complete, or some items may not be required for several days.

Shortages are caused mainly by inventory inaccuracies, poor scheduling, unreported scrap, or supplier issues. Inventory inaccuracies are difficult to control, since the perpetual inventory relies on the accuracy of the information from various sources. As stated in Chapter 8, a robust cycle-counting effort is required to identify and resolve the component inaccuracies.

The pull system of issuing supplier requirements is the best and most accurate system of identifying shortages. There are different methods of implementing pull systems. Although the Toyota Kanban[3] system is considered one of the best systems for stock replenishment, people must move Kanban cards in the system. This is a drawback, because cards can be lost. Chapter 19 discusses a better process that is visual and does not rely on Kanban card movements.

SUPPLIER CHARGE-BACK SYSTEM

In order to enforce the need to obtain quality products on time, the downtime charge-back can be an effective tool. Many companies have adopted a process of charging suppliers for downtime that they have incurred due to lack of product on a timely basis.

Suppliers need to adopt the same level of urgency for maintaining on-time shipments as manufacturing plants do to their customers. Debiting for downtime is a reasonable practice, as long as the plant does not abuse it. As with all charges, it makes sense to obtain the supplier's agreement prior to sending an invoice for downtime charges. The downtime note should contain the time the production process was stopped, the number of people that continued to be paid, and when the production process started again.

Some suppliers have excellent communications that allow customers to know when there are potential supply issues. Others do not communicate as well, which creates havoc with planning. Suppliers that do not communicate the potential issues or missed shipments need to understand the importance of communicating to the plant.

One method of improving supplier communications with the plant is to hold a supplier/plant development meeting on a regular schedule. At the meeting, the plant can present its expectations, and the suppliers have a chance to discuss any issues that they might have.

If there is nothing specified in the purchase order regarding capacity and an agreed schedule increase percentage, disputes concerning the responsibility for downtime are bound to arise. Even if the purchase order does not discuss downtime compensation, the plant should have a detailed policy. The best practice is to construct a letter of intent that specifies the intent to charge suppliers for downtime incidents relating to supply issues. In addition, the letter should specify a grace period: the amount of time allotted before the debit is charged to the supplier. The letter should specify the dollar-per-hour rate and any other potential charge-back dollars, such as an administration fee. Suppliers that are notified up front are more prepared to manage a supply issue and its potential cost impacts. Suppliers also should be given a specified deadline date on which to contest any pending debit before the debit is created.

The process of writing a debit for downtime should be controlled and managed by a simple form with the supplier name, downtime date, total time down, number of people affected, and reason for downtime. Paperwork detailing the on-order position must prove that the supplier was clearly delinquent, and net change information must show that the plant was within any accepted change guidelines. Suppliers will need to present paperwork that substantiates their point of view and indicate the reason(s) for not being charged. EDI or Web records that can refute or prove the charges should provide the foundation for any dispute.

One drawback to the debit system is that some suppliers refuse to ship components to the plant after they have received a debit. In this case, it takes some negotiation with suppliers to show them that they were in fact the cause of lost time.

A supplier may refuse to accept debits for downtime or excess freight. This poses an issue for the plant since this type of supplier is usually one that produces a unique product that is difficult to obtain from an alternate source.

CUSTOMER-MANDATED SUPPLIERS

Customer-mandated suppliers are not always the best scenario for a plant to manage because they can be difficult to deal with. Mandated suppliers do have an advantage for the plant. Since the customer has established the formal relations with the mandated supplier, any supply issues become issues for the customer to deal with. A quick phone call to the customer with a concern about a selected supplier usually achieves the desired results.

NOTES

1. A "firm planned order" is an order for materials that is entered by a planner or changed from an MRP-suggested order to a fixed order.
2. "Gross requirements" are the total requirements for finished product generated by EDI and/or planning orders for shipping. Component gross requirements are generated from the EDI, forecast, shipping lines, or firm planned orders that entered at the finished good level.
3. "Kanban" is a system for replenishment triggered by using pre-printed cards as a build signal. Kanban cards usually contain the part number, quantity, and supplying department.

CHAPTER 10

PLANNING PARAMETERS

Planning parameters are used in the materials requirement planning (MRP) system to create a particular action or function for the components that are used to set the MRP guidelines for components, work in progress (WIP), and finished goods. Many different planning parameters in computer systems determine how planning and control systems work for ordering, manufacturing, receiving, and shipping.

For component ordering, planning parameters consist of safety stock calculations, time periods, transit time, purchasing lead time, and plant lead time. Planning parameters are so critical to the MRP process that when abused or used incorrectly, they directly contribute to shortages, large imbalances, poor release schedules, and a host of other problems that complicate the planning process.

The best practice, described in more detail later, is to limit the number of planning parameters that affect a particular process, such as the releasing process. For example, a plant that has a continuous manufacturing process with one-piece flow as a goal should never use lead times at any level in the bill of materials except for the lowest level.

MAKE-TO-ORDER PLANTS

Plants that produce make-to-order items may need to consider lead times at all steps of the process. For example, a one-of-a-kind product made for an aircraft assembly may have an extensive process and consist of components that are manufactured in a series of steps. In this case, a lead time with every step of the process may be a best, and an unavoidable, practice.

The plant needs to determine the minimum carrying quantity on hand for all components and finished goods. If the plant is using the MRP computer system to generate releases to suppliers, system parameters must be set properly in order to avert shortages or overstock. The computer system will generate minimum balances based on parameters set in the system for a specified period of time using gross requirements and the number of carrying days. Gross requirements are the sum of all orders in the system; they can be manually entered orders or system-generated orders over a particular period that is specified by a planning parameter.

CONTROLLING PLANNING PARAMETERS

The minimum balance calculation is determined by dividing the sum of the gross requirements in a specified period by the number of days in the chosen period and then multiplying the result by the number of carrying days. For example, if the selected gross requirement is 30 days and the sum of all of the requirements in this 30-day period is 9,000, then the daily requirement is 9,000 divided by 30, or 300. The system then calculates the minimum balance using the carrying parameter times 300. If the carrying parameter is two days, then the minimum balance in this calculation is 600.

The MRP system launches releases for quantities of materials based on gross requirements set in weeks and ensures that the amount of material ordered maintains minimum balances. For example, if the minimum balance for a component is calculated at 1,000 pieces, there are 500 pieces in stock, and the first planning week of demand[1] is 1,000, then 1,500 pieces are required. The release launched to the supplier will be 1,500 pieces, which is the difference between the balance on hand (500) and the gross requirements in the first planning week (1,000), and the minimum balance.

Lead-time planning parameters are used to generate the release dates to suppliers and are used internally to add time to build product. It is not advisable to use lead time to build product if there is a continuous operation in the plant since this calculation will increase the inventory.

The due date of component releases generated to suppliers is backed up by the total of all the lead times attached to the particular component. For example, if there is a lead time of 5 days set for the finished good, 3 days for a WIP level, and 5 days for the component level, the total lead time is equal to 13 days. The requirements are released with a delivery date of 13 days before the finished good due date in the MRP system. Misunderstanding the use of lead times is one cause of high inventory dollars. Lead time should be used only at the component level where there is a continuous process, and it should represent the true time it takes to ship the component from the supplier to the receipt date into the plant.

The release generation[2] from MRP is usually set for a particular day of the week. MRP usually is generated in the evening, when there is full access to the data and few changes are likely to arise. MRP explosions[3] for component requirements are generated through the bill of materials from the highest levels down to the lowest levels. Once the release generation occurs, the component requirements are updated on a part-by-part basis, and new schedules are created. For example, if part A takes 3 of part ABC and part B takes 2 of part ABC, the computer system will automatically multiply the gross requirements for A times 3 for ABC and add the demand from B times 2 for ABC. The net result is the demand for part ABC. Depending on how the planning parameters are set for part ABC, the releases will reflect the delivery or ship date of the product required by day or week. If the inventory is inaccurate, it is not a good practice to issue daily releases to suppliers, as suppliers will begin to regard the releases as unreliable. In such cases, there is a high probability that there will be supply arguments stemming from release integrity.

Releases can be generated to show the ship date from the supplier or the delivery date into the plant. If the supplier is paying for the freight, then the release date sent to the supplier should be the date that the plant expects to receive the components. If the plant is paying for the freight, then the release date sent to the supplier should be the supplier ship date. The advantage of generating a ship date is that it is clear when the item must leave the supplier, and it can be easily traced.

Although the ship date versus the receive date makes the most sense, this practice is not generally followed. Most plants release requirements with due dates. The bottom line is that the expected delivery dates must allow enough time to receive the components and manufacture the product continuously.

To receive components on a timely basis, the computer system planning parameters for setting lead times must be adjusted properly for the transit time and the frequency of shipments. A planning parameter should govern the day of week on which a delivery or shipment is expected. For example, if the component is scheduled to be shipped on Mondays and Thursdays from a supplier, then the calculation for the quantity to be shipped and day of shipment will be adjusted to meet this delivery profile.

Several other planning parameters may be used to govern the release strategy. Most suppliers ship components in standard package quantities. The MRP system has a parameter than can be preset for each component's standard package quantity. When releases to the supplier are generated from the MRP system, the releases will reflect multiples of the package size that has been entered into the system. A drawback to this system occurs when the supplier's package size exceeds the plant's daily inventory goal. Standard package quantities are essential for pull systems to work effectively because most scanning systems are used to scan boxes, not the quantities in the boxes.

Order policy parameters are also available in MRP systems. Depending on the MRP system, there may be a multitude of choices. For example, an order policy instructs MRP to add all the demand for a specified period and then generate one release for this time. This particular order policy is good for small-dollar items that have a very low usage over a specific period. For some reason, plants do not use most of the available

EXHIBIT **10.1**   *Most Frequent Planning Parameters for Component Ordering*

Period Order Quantity—Adds all of the demand for a period and places a bulk release for the total.

Multiple Order Quantity—Releases are generated in standard package quantities.

Single Order Quantity—Releases are generated in any quantity.

---

planning parameters that can help control and monitor inventory. However, such parameters are available.

As with any chosen system of control, planning parameters that are used incorrectly can lead to an inventory excess or shortfall. Before using a planning parameter, the planning department must clearly understand the outcome. Exhibit 10.1 presents some of the most common planning parameters for controlling order quantities from suppliers.

NOTES

1. "Demand" is the sum of all orders in a particular week and any amount required to maintain the minimum balance.
2. "Component release generation" is the calculation of requirements based on the gross requirements, lead times, and safety stock levels to derive the dates and quantities need from suppliers.
3. An "explosion" is the process of generating demand using MRP to calculate the requirements.

CHAPTER 11

ELECTRONIC DATA INTERCHANGE

Electronic data interchange (EDI) is the widely accepted practice of electronically transmitting releases to suppliers and receiving releases from customers. EDI therefore is an integral part of the materials management process.

To ensure that the customer demand is correct, EDI must be received and transmitted correctly. All computer systems should have a fallout report that is generated each time EDI is received into the plant. The fallout report shows the errors that must be reviewed and corrected on a daily basis in order to ensure the correctness of the data received.

Some fallout on the report may not need to be addressed immediately. This fallout may be caused by the customer sending the incorrect level or incorrect part number. New product numbers generally appear on the error report when the customer transmits releases before the plant has created the internal part number that links to the customer number.

A failure to understand and correct the EDI errors from customers will most likely result in charging the plant for the customer premium freight and possibly downtime charges.

Depending on the computer system and the interface with the customer's system, the data required to receive releases properly can be simple or complicated. Most materials requirement planning (MRP) computer systems have a series of data fields, sometimes on multiple screens, that must be filled in properly in order to receive the customer EDI releases. A failure or lack of one data input parameter might cause the computer system to reject customer EDI for a particular line item.

The best practice is to establish a procedure that clearly shows all fields that must be filled in properly and the criteria for filling in the fields.

EDI from customers may come in several forms: daily and weekly releases, planning requirements, and comments. Some planning groups refer to daily and weekly releases as 862 and 830 releases.

Customer releases are sent to the company Electronic/Web mailbox. From the company mailbox, the releases are translated into the receiving company's computer system. Several manual steps via various data screens may be involved upon receiving the releases into the company mailbox and translating the releases into the company computer. Most companies, however, have programmed this process so that no manual input is required.

A failure to retrieve customer releases will result in old and possibly inaccurate data in the system from the previous week that has not been cleared out of MRP. Usually a set of planning parameters governs release information for each finished part number, since different customers may have different EDI releasing strategies. Therefore, it is extremely important to understand how to select the planning parameters correctly. There must be a fail-safe measure that alerts the materials department if the EDI has not transmitted properly into the MRP system.

Along with EDI, most all systems communicate the cumulative balances between sender and receiver. If the cumulative balances do not agree, they must be reconciled before making the next shipment.

If no correction is made in the cumulative balances, the amount to be shipped will be overstated or understated by the amount of the cumulative disagreement. The result is usually a scramble to make parts and try to ship them on time.

Someone should be assigned the task of managing the cumulative balances to ensure that the computer is processing the correct information. Correcting the cumulative balances can be simple or complicated, depending on the ability of both sender and receiver to provide historical information on shipments and receipts. Some customers maintain Web sites that are accessible to the supplying plants showing audit trails of product received and rejected. A comparative analysis of the customer's Web site information and the supplying plant's shipping information can be easily obtained, compared, and then corrected.

A system of electronic communication and tracking is the best process for managing release information. The major drawback of facsimile releases is that they must be manually entered into the system. It is also more difficult to track the cumulative shipment quantities using manual releases since there is no automatic function to add the cumulative balances.

With facsimile releases, a major issue is determining what is in transit that the customer has not counted in the manual release generated to the plant. The plant needs to deduct the amount of the shipments in transit from the customers' manual release quantities if the customer has not taken the in-transit amounts into consideration in their latest release generation. The best practice of managing manual releases is to assign line numbers to the releases by date and then assign the line number to the shipments.

Another good feature of the electronic release is the ability to quickly compare net changes from one release to the next. The tracking of net release changes is invaluable in providing information about inventory excesses or shortages. At times the information from tracking the net changes can resolve disputes with customers or suppliers. For example, if there is an agreement that releases can be increased by 20 percent maximum and the customer increases releases 30 percent, causing overtime and excessive freight for the plant, the net changes of the EDI releases will prove the point.

Exhibit 11.1 is a typical process flow of release information from suppliers.

EXHIBIT **11.1** *Process Flow for the Delivery of Customer Product*

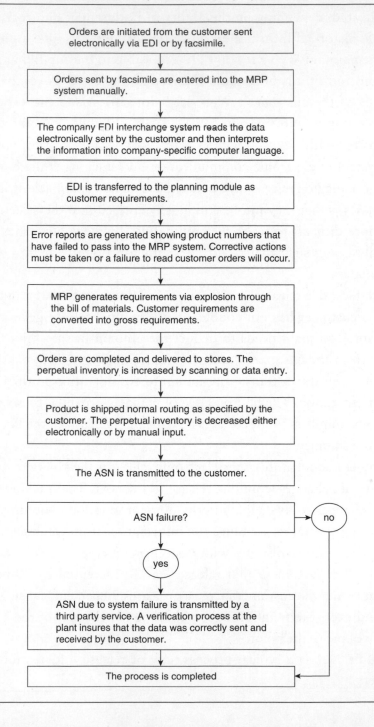

CHAPTER 12

MATERIALS CONTROL GRAPHS AND REPORTS

Materials control reports and graphs should be designed to show the progress toward obtaining company goals and objectives that have been assigned to the materials department. The reports and graphs should accurately depict the department's progress in achieving goals and objectives.

Materials presentations should include, at minimum, cycle-count accuracy, on-time customer ratings, premium freight, and inventory days or turns to plan. Some top managers request turns of inventory as opposed to inventory days; however, from a materials planning perspective, days on hand has more meaning. Exhibit 12.1 shows two typical inventory graphs for reporting inventory dollars.

ON-TIME DELIVERY

The on-time delivery graph needs to be based entirely on customers' ratings. An attached action plan for each issue that has negatively affected the rating should be provided with an assigned name and a due date. The graph should be simple, showing the rating for the last 12 rolling months and the separate details of the customer rating if the customer presents its rating points in categories. Exhibit 12.2 is a typical graph of customer on-time delivery. It may be helpful to list actions to

EXHIBIT **12.1** *Typical Inventory Graphs*

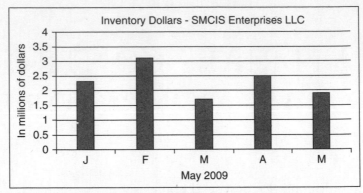

This graph shows inventory dollars on hand.

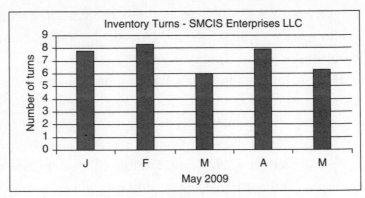

This graph shows the inventory turns.

improve the customer on-time-delivery in a separate section directly under the graph.

PREMIUM FREIGHT

Graphs for premium freight or excess freight have little significance if they are not consistent between plants in an organization. A clear method of recording excess freight needs to be established in order to keep the graphs from one plant to another comparable. A definition of

EXHIBIT **12.2**   *Typical Customer Complaint Graph*

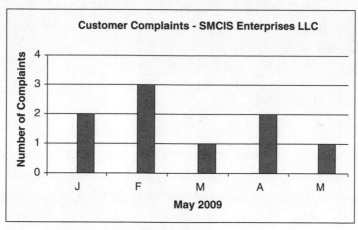

Incorrect shipping destination
4/13   tag - see 7D written May 6th
One of several graphs that could be used to show the customer rating.

excess freight and premium needs to be decided on for the corporation as a whole.

Usually premium freight is the cost of a shipment that was expedited, by either a land or an air carrier. Excess freight is usually the net freight extra expense incurred by using a carrier other than the normal designated carrier at an increased cost. For example, if the corporation has a contract with UPS, the cost of a shipment is normally $50, and a non-approved overnight carrier was used at a cost of $60, then the excess freight is $10. Most companies do not track excess freight, although doing so is important in order to gain a full understanding of any freight management system and to create a charge back if possible.

INVENTORY ACCURACY

The inventory accuracy graph or cycle-count graph is difficult to design accurately to depict what has transpired. Although the data collection method explained in the "Cycle Counting" section below is unconventional, it is a more accurate method of capturing the inventory accuracy over the long range and will reveal components with a history of issues.

CYCLE COUNTING

The best cycle-count graph is one that contains ongoing information that is constantly updated from one cycle-count date to the next. The most important part of any cycle count is the number of parts lost per day stated in pieces or a percentage over time. The data collected from many cycle counts for the same part over a six-month period or longer can help identify problem parts prone to shrinkage. For example, component A was cycle-counted on June 4. On June 4, an adjustment was made to the perpetual inventory which will serve as the baseline. Twenty-five days later another cycle count revealed a loss of 2,000 pieces. That equates to 80 pieces per day, 2,000/25. To determine if this is an acceptable number, divide the 80 pieces per day average by the average number of components used daily. If in our example the plant consumes 8,000 pieces per day on average, then the cycle count loss is 1 percent, 80/8,000. The loss of 1 percent may or may not be acceptable for the plant.

This cycle-counting analysis method can be used to identify the components by part numbers that have the highest shrinkage. Once the analysis is performed, measures can be taken in the materials requirement planning (MRP) system to prevent the shrinkages from becoming line shortages.

The inventory days on hand graph usually is calculated by using accounting data from the cost of goods sold and the number of accounting days in a particular month. Most companies use the current month's cost of sales in the calculation.

Some companies use the next month's estimated cost of sales to compute inventory turns, based on the idea that the inventory on hand at the end of the month is used for the next month's production

EXHIBIT **12.3**   *Cycle-Count Dollars Adjusted*

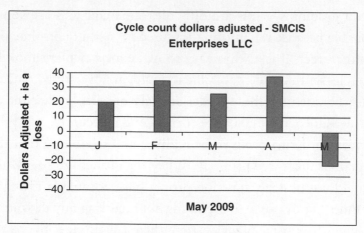

The gain in May is due to a bill of materials error.

and sales. If a company chooses to use estimated data from the next month to calculate inventory days, it should be standard practice to go back and recalculate the numbers based on the actual numbers. This must be done because an overforecasted sales plan that is used in the turn calculation equates to a turn number that is skewed favorably.

Exhibit 12.3 presents a cycle-counting graph.

PRESENTATIONS

Putting charts, graphs, and Pareto charts into the proper perspective is not necessarily an easy task. It is, however, in the company's best interests to set guidelines for the entire corporation that do not leave room for plant interpretation of the data, especially if the information is to be compared from one plant to the next.

Best-in-class materials presentations should include data that is factual and can be supported by documents or system-generated reports. For example, if one plant includes the in-transit materials from non-U.S. producers as physical inventory, all plants should follow suit.

INTERPLANT GRADING SYSTEMS

Interplant grading systems are difficult to manage and are sometimes questionable because the information used to measure on-time delivery is often incorrect. It is always easy to make a sister plant look bad by sending releases that are impossible to build, are overstated, and change constantly. Sometimes these grades are very unreliable since the criteria used to measure performance are corrupt and inaccurate.

Interplant ordering needs to be realistic and reliable so that the supplying plant is measured properly. When the ratings are so low that the plant could not possibly function properly, performing a rating simply wastes time. For example, if a plant is not incurring any downtime and is supplying their sister plant on-time then it is not feasible to rate the sister plant as a non-performer. A supplier release should not be considered as past due if there is no immediate need for the component—in other words, a shortage in the plant.

The better alternative to managing releases from a sister facility is not to send releases at all. Since everyone should be using the same MRP system, linked plants should be able to manage the requirements themselves. The receiving plant needs to ensure two things:

1. The inventory is accurate all of the time.
2. Minimum and maximum quantities are consistent and updated regularly.

Graphs and charts that depict how well the materials department is functioning must be measured from data that can be supported by paper or electronic documentation. The best graphs and charts depict the details necessary to show what is occurring, who is assigned to correct the issues, and when the issues are going to be corrected.

CHAPTER 13

OBSOLESCENCE

Materials control needs to assign the highest priority to managing obsolescence in plants without incurring an excessive amount of obsolete inventory. Some obsolescence issues are caused by a simple lack of communication between plant and customer and between plant and suppliers. Other obsolescence issues are caused by a general failure to manage releases and inventory properly.

BALANCE-OUT OF PRODUCT OR COMPONENTS

Before starting a balance-out or engineering change, it is always better to discuss the options with both the customer and the supply base. Agreements established before there is an issue will make the process go smoother.

To begin with, the customer must provide the final balance-out numbers in some form of written notice. If the customer and the providing plant can agree on a final production number, everyone will benefit, and the ownership for the remaining materials will be easily identified. If customers provide a balance-out range, they need to understand that the plant will cover the high end. If customers end the program before the high-end number is reached, they will bear the cost.

Electronic releases may provide the data required to plan the balance-out of product properly since they generally contain a high fabrication and a high raw material number that the plant needs to purchase and build.

The high fabrication number is the number the customer allows the plant to have in process beyond the final balance-out number. The high raw material number is the amount of product that the customer agrees to pay for raw materials that may be on order. These numbers may or may not agree with the final cumulative number since they are meant to serve as protection for changes or extensions in the planning process. Customers will have to pay for inventory that remains for the balance-out numbers that they issue.

Numbers can be changed in any computer system. The company must determine a method of locking in the highest numbers that have been transmitted by the customer during the given balance-out period. The highest numbers will protect the company from a downward trend in releases from the customer.

PREVENTING OBSOLESCENCE

The materials requirement planning (MRP) system may have controls that can be used to prevent obsolescence once the final numbers are known. Start and end dates for components may be entered into most systems. When used properly, these numbers will signal the end of component ordering and start a new or revised component level (provided a new part number is assigned). Use of these fields can have good results; the danger lies is in not maintaining changes in the computer system when the end date is revised or there is an inventory adjustment.

Using revision numbers when components are revised is not a good plan if the computer system cannot record both part numbers and revision numbers. When revision numbers are used with systems that are not designed to accommodate them, the inventory gets mixed in the system.

Many companies fail to manage the inventory properly in the final stages of a balance-out. The issue behind failures to balance-out materials properly usually relates to using the computer system inventory without physically verifying the counts. There is only one way to manage a balance-out of a product line with many components and subassemblies correctly: Physically manage the inventory on a daily or weekly basis. In addition, any subassembly work must be contained in a specific area and the inventory of subassemblies must be stored properly for counting ease.

Using the customer electronic data interchange (EDI) is the best way to manage a balance-out number for the finished product. If there is no EDI capability from the customer, a written release should be used to enter the requirements into the MRP system manually. The written release must be signed by the customer and indicate the final numbers to be produced and shipped. The plant's failure to receive a final release in writing may lead to problems when it attempts to collect money for in-process excess or remaining components.

The governing parameters that add safety inventory to the finished goods, work-in-process levels, and components should be eliminated near the completion of the project so that the system does not generate materials that will not be used.

The best practice is to remove all of the planning parameters that add inventory to the perpetual inventory at the appropriate time. A cutoff number for the finished goods should then be established, and the finished goods should be manually planned using firm planned orders so that the MRP system does not move or add to the requirements.

Action is a key word for avoiding obsolescence from suppliers. A formal letter to the supplier indicating the balance-out number for the raw parts and the finished components is appropriate and essential to a successful balance-out. The letter should state that the balance-out number provided takes precedence over the EDI release numbers.

Although the final numbers are communicated to the suppliers via EDI, there is a chance that suppliers may ship beyond the final number. There must be a way to stop a shipment of material that exceeds the final balance-out number to avoid a receipt of unplanned material. Deleting or nullifying the open purchase order in the MRP system will prevent the entering of additional materials received in the MRP.

Plants using bar code scanning may not be able to rely on the MRP system to flag overordering. Close management is the only way to control a balance-out for a component using bar code scanning or visual pull systems.

Since most pull systems use scanning equipment for releasing components, the number of available scans for releasing can be reduced or eliminated as the life of the part being replaced nears completion. A manual daily monitoring system that alerts the person scanning that the component is being phased out must exist as well.

Plants with perpetual inventory accuracy problems are prone to large obsolescence issues. It is important to cycle-count the components on a regular schedule, especially near the end of a program's life. Daily counts will help ensure that there are no last-minute shortages.

Deviations in releases vacillating up and down will lead to confusion and possibly a dispute over ownership of remaining inventories. Therefore, releases to suppliers at or near the end of a program must be kept consistent and smooth so that there is no confusion or questions about the final numbers ordered.

AVOIDING SUPPLIER AND CUSTOMER OBSOLESCENCE

As the time for the final production numbers draws near, there should be a concerted effort to ensure that all materials that are rejected are processed and returned to the suppliers on a timely basis. Any materials that are manufactured internally and placed on hold should be processed for final disposition well ahead of the program's end.

Customers that frequently change balance-out numbers should be made aware of the consequences of their actions. The best and only practice is to lock in the customer at a final balance-out number. If the customer increases the balance-out number, shortages from suppliers with long lead times might ensue. It is important to inform customers of the longest lead-time items from the supplier base in order to avoid some unfriendly communications later down the road. Clearly, the interaction from the customer to the plant materials department must be firsthand and then from the plant materials department to the plants supplier.

In the case of obsolescence for any reason other than the plant's own doing, a clear method of recovering the money for the product must be available. Most customers have procedures and timelines for collecting obsolescence payments. Care must be taken to adhere to the customers' schedules. Once a claim is approved, customers may authorize the plant to scrap the product or ship it to a storage facility of the customers' choosing.

Exhibit 13.1 is a typical flowchart of the steps that may be used for new or replacement product. These steps are generally effective in ensuring that there is a minimal amount to obsolescence due to changes.

EXHIBIT **13.1** *New or Replacement Product Changes*

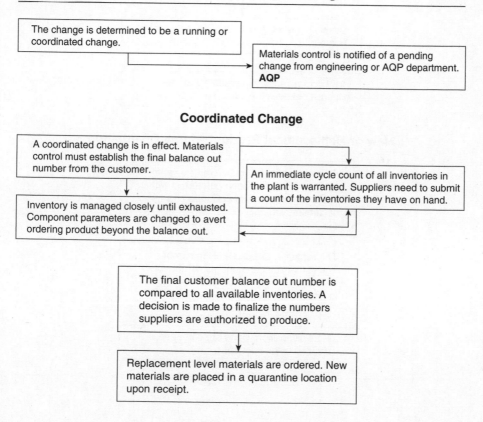

(*Continued*)

EXHIBIT 13.1 *Continued*

New or Replacement Product—Running Change

The suppliers are notified in writing of the change and they are requested to provide inventory balance out numbers.

↓

A running change is noted. Cycle all parts that are changing. Equalize all components being changed. Materials control needs to establish the final balance out number with the customer based upon the materials available.

↓

The final accumulated balance out number is communicated to the customer utilizing the maximum amount of inventory dollars.

↓

Suppliers are notified of the final balance out number.

↓

Plant scraps remaining materials at their expense or keeps the components for service.

New or Replacement Product—Final Disposition

A claim for obsolescence credit is written for items that have been purchased within customer authorizations. Supporting documents are on file.

↓

The customer assigns a claim number. The authorized components need to be labeled with the claim number and placed in a restricted area.

↓

Final disposition: Parts are scrapped or shipped to the customer.

CHAPTER 14

PHYSICAL INVENTORIES

Why do companies place so much emphasis on physical invento-ries in order to verify perpetual inventories? The answer is the lack of trust in the systems that are in place to capture the value of the computer inventory on a day-to-day basis compared to the ledger.

Some companies can resolve major inventory losses by scheduling monthly or bimonthly physical inventories. This is an obvious cost expense in labor and lost production time that plants should avoid. Most companies that frequently count the inventory with complete physicals are already overextending the labor force with long working hours.

A solid corrective action plan needs to be devised and implemented in order to eliminate frequent perpetual company wide inventories. Major problems in inept receiving, shipping, scrap, bills of materials, produc-tion reporting, and cycle-counting practices can make an inventory dys-functional. Each one of the major inventory issues can be corrected with an action plan and follow-up.

In a well-maintained and accurate perpetual inventory, there may be a downside to taking a physical inventory if the physical inventory is not planned and executed properly. The posting of a physical inventory that is less accurate than the perpetual inventory can have a damaging effect causing plant shortages, or creating releases for materials that are not required.

Taking a physical inventory correctly is not optional. The foremost issue to deal with is selecting the proper individuals to perform the inventory. Personnel must understand the importance of counting correctly and ensuring that the part numbers are verified.

Most of the inventory staff should be plant auditors who focus on selecting, reviewing, and correcting a large percentage of inventory tags in a given area prior to posting. Creating groups of personnel to ensure part number and quantity correctness is as essential as selecting a qualified auditing staff.

There must exist a set of instructions that covers all aspects of the inventory. All departments that have any influence on the perpetual inventory should be included in the instructions.

Receiving needs to complete all transactions before the start of the inventory, and the docks should be locked from receiving additional materials. If a shipment must be received into the plant, the materials should be quarantined and flagged "after inventory."

A shipping cutoff time is sometimes more difficult to accomplish. If shipments need go to the customer during the inventory, the best practice is to load the trailers in advance.

During the inventory, movement of materials in the plant should be completely restricted. This may be difficult to accomplish if departments have to keep making product due to time constraints. Any department that needs to continue manufacturing during the physical inventory must ensure that the raw materials required are in the department before the inventory begins.

A well-planned, organized and timely physical taking of the inventory is essential to getting the plant back into full production on time. The best practices are to ensure that the subassembly processes are held to a minimum. If the process or small assembly lines can be cleared of components, the duration of time spent in the assembly cells will be limited since there will be less materials on the factory floor to count.

If the plant has a warehouse or a storeroom, it makes the most sense to send back all unopened boxes from the assembly lines. The less material on the manufacturing floor, the quicker and smoother the counting will go. In addition, fewer people are required to perform the physical inventory. Proper planning and consolidation of components will reduce the number of hours spent counting.

Although the total inventory in dollars in a physical inventory may be within a very acceptable amount, there is no guarantee of acceptance by the planners on a part-by-part basis. Shortages may result if a physical inventory is posted that is much different on a part-by-part basis from the perpetual inventory. A comparison with the physical inventory numbers on a part-by-part basis must satisfy the planners that are responsible for the replenishment and control of the accuracy.

INVENTORY RECONCILIATION

The materials department must decide how much time to spend reconciling the physical to the perpetual inventory to ensure that there are no surprise shortages after the inventory is posted.

To the materials department, it should not matter if the total value of the variance from the perpetual inventory to the physical parts counted is $100 or $10,000 as long as the parts counted do not deviate too far from the perpetual inventory, especially gains. Any gains in the physical versus the perpetual inventory are candidates for shortages when it is discovered later that the physical count was incorrect. Large gains should be noted and investigated thoroughly.

Accuracy percentages calculated by taking the perpetual (book) numbers versus the physical numbers counted are poor measures of inventory accuracy. Such calculations generate information that really does not depict the inventory accuracy since it does not consider overall product usage over a stated period. Take the example of a physical count for part A, which is 80,000 pieces, when the book is 70,000 pieces. Part A has a value of $.001 each. Ten thousand pieces are to be written off the books at a value of $100; however, on a component average usage basis, the loss is 14 percent, which is not acceptable and a planner should request for a recount of the item.

What does the 14 percent adjustment really represent? It is not a good measure of accuracy because the equation does not include any time duration and quantity used. A 14 percent loss on a component over a year before the last count is much different from a 14 percent adjustment on the same component that was cycle-counted the day before.

Another view is to consider that over 8,500,000 of these parts are consumed in a period from physical count to physical count. During the year, there were inventory count losses of 60,000 pieces. Taking the 60,000 and dividing it by the annual usage equates to a loss of 7/10 of a percent. A 7/10 percent loss is most likely acceptable, over a time span of a year compared to one point in time that would result in a higher percentage of shrink. Taking the same number of a 60,000-piece loss and comparing it to the current inventory on hand, the percentage may be much different. If at the physical inventory there were only 200,000 pieces on the books, then the physical inventory accuracy would be 30 percent. This number is cause for alarm, but in reality over the production of one year, the true loss is 7/10 of a percent. True inventory accuracy should be measured over time and quantity used, not at a particular point in time.

Many companies have adopted a policy that allows the waiving of a physical inventory. The challenge is to determine the reasoning behind not taking a physical inventory. The decision to take a physical inventory should always be based on the accuracy of the part numbers and not solely on the dollar values.

A selection of a number of parts to audit for accuracy is a good starting point for determining if a physical inventory is required. The number of parts should be selected randomly and based on a percentage of dollars versus the total perpetual dollars. There should also be a review of the cycle-counting process, the accuracy of the counts taken, and verifiable evidence showing the action plans implemented to correct faults in the data input/output systems.

There should always be concerted efforts to prevent materials from arriving to the plant just before the physical inventory, if they are not required immediately. Fewer materials at physical inventory are advantageous to the counters as well as the materials group that needs to reconcile the physical to the perpetual inventory. The less material that is in receiving, inspection, rejected, or on hold in the plant, the more effective the inventory is going to be.

If plants completely clean up work areas, organize the inventory, return unopened boxes to stores, reduce work in process, and empty out assembly lines of components, there is no reason why an inventory cannot be completed in half a day.

CHAPTER 15

RECEIVING

The six elements of receiving are:

1. Customer returns
2. Receiving discrepancy report (RDR) process
3. Inspection
4. Verification of receipt
5. Damage control
6. Audit

A well-organized and efficient receiving department is essential to good materials control. There needs to be a well-defined process for receiving materials from suppliers, processing paperwork, and transferring the goods to a point of use or stores site.

A well-organized receiving department will have little or no materials waiting to be moved to a storage site for any reason. Timing and accuracy of data entry are the key elements to proper receiving and quick movement of materials. In addition, promptly entering data into the computer system will allow the visibility required for managing the inventory properly. A large backlog of receiving paperwork for data entry will affect the ability to view what is on hand and may prompt unnecessary phone calls to suppliers.

Most companies have developed skip-lot inspection techniques that allow for the quick movement of materials. Suppliers are asked to self-certify their components so that the receiving plant does not have to inspect every lot received. After receiving components from suppliers, the lot is verified for inspection requirements. The lot is then inspected or moved to the storage site immediately.

The best receiving systems are those that are capable of printing a receiving label with the part number, the lot number, and the location of where the part is to be delivered. The printed labels are attached to every box or container. Generally, this system is used in conjunction with bar code scanning and/or receiving inspection software.

There is receiving inspection software available that will allow the printing of inspection/part number labels only when the component is skipped for inspection or no inspection is required. By not printing a label, the system indicates that the product needs to be inspected. Once the product is inspected, the quality department releases the system to print the inspection labels.

REVIEW OF RECEIVING PRACTICES

A general walk-through of a facility's receiving and inspection areas can bring to light any issues in the inspection and receiving process. Preservation of materials is of the utmost importance. Broken skids, crushed boxes, improperly stacked containers, and poor general housekeeping are signs that issues in receiving need to be addressed.

Verification of the receiving dates on the materials is a good indication of how well the area is being managed. If any goods are stale dated, there may be issues with timely processing of paperwork or inspection timeliness.

It is not enough to walk through and visually observe the receiving area; there may be an ominous pile of receiving paperwork lingering in a bin somewhere. Receiving paperwork may be backed up for two reasons:

1. There may not be sufficient staff to enter the transactions into the system on a timely basis.
2. There may be issues with matching open receiving lines (they have been canceled or modified) to the supplier's shipment.

Neither of these issues is difficult to manage, yet each can get out of control quickly.

With the advent of reducing inventories to the bare minimum, the best practice is to get receiving completed into the system within two hours of receipt.

VERIFICATION PROCESS

A verification process is needed to ensure that the data entered in the system is correct. The simplest practice is to generate a report of the information entered and then verify it to the paperwork. A better method, bar coding, is described in Chapter 20.

Some companies use a log of numbers that they assign to each packing slip entered into the system. This practice is acceptable, but a better practice is to use the packing slip number or another approved reference number listed on the packing slip.

A detailed work instruction must list which numbers on a packing slip to use for cross-reference so that there is no confusion or difficulty in matching the accounting invoice to the entry into the system. Systems designed to pay via the entry of packing slips into the computer system rely on a good cross-reference number to ensure that the supplier and the company can match the billing properly.

Lost packing slips can be an issue in a plant, especially if plant labels are not used to check in materials. The most common reason for losing packing slips is when inexperienced personnel working second or third shifts receive parts and misplace or fail to retrieve the paperwork before sending the parts into the plant for use.

A good way to minimize issues with lost packing slips is to have a detailed work instruction that shows how the material should be handled and to provide proper training.

A good method to determine whether receipts are being entered into the system properly is to generate a weekly report of the cumulative balances between plant and supplier. Any discrepancy found in these cumulative balances may be reason to suspect that receiving has not been performed properly or that a packing slip has been lost. The supplier needs to be contacted and the accumulated difference needs to be corrected with a copy of a packing slip from the supplier if necessary.

Packing slips that seem to get the least attention are those that involve maintenance and repair orders (MRO)[1] items. MRO items often get hand-carried into a facility, drop-shipped, or taken by people who have the product sent to them. It is difficult to stop the process of drop-shipping and premature pickup, especially since many people may be involved with ordering products.

Providing a designated spot for all MRO items to be placed is a good practice, provided the packing slips are removed immediately and processed by receiving. Suppliers that hand-carry product to a department other than receiving should be advised that the packing slip is the instrument that initiates payment for product received. Without it, there is a guaranteed delay of payment. To go one step further, suppliers should not be allowed to deliver parts directly to anyone in the plant.

Bar code scanning is the best practice for receiving items into inventory. This method generally eliminates the errors made with manual entries. However, bar code scanning will not resolve the issue of lost packing slips or parts being delivered to the production area without being scanned.

BEST PRACTICE

Another process that is gaining popularity in the manufacturing world is to receive goods by advance shipping notification (ASN). The ASN sent from suppliers shows what they have in transit. Upon receipt of the goods to the dock, the ASN can be processed into the materials requirement planning (MRP) system as the receipt of goods for payment. The ASN can be used to update the perpetual inventory. With this process, the company can send an acknowledgment to the supplier's ASN with any count corrections. The ability to send ASNs resides in the sender's MRP system. There is no reason why companies that use an MRP system cannot send ASNs. In this method, each container

EXHIBIT 15.1 *Receiving Discrepancy Report Example*

Date Received:	PSN (Packing Slip Number):
Supplier Name or number:	
Part Number:	
PSQ# (Packing Slip Quantity#):	Actual:
Count Discrepancy:	
Quantity Damaged:	Photo attached:
Incorrect Label:	Photo attached:
Incorrect Packaging:	Photo attached:
Photographs:	

is scanned, and that scan is matched to the ASN line to verify the actual count received.

Every company needs to have a robust system for managing customer returns. Managing returns should never be a complex issue, but some companies fail to implement sound practices. An RDR should be in a format that is readily available for the receiving person to complete. The old saying that a "picture paints a thousand words" applies to items that are nonconforming. Exhibit 15.1 is a simple RDR form.

DAMAGED MATERIALS

RDRs should be used for damaged materials that are received. There is nothing more conclusive than attaching a photograph of a damaged product while it is still on the carrier. It is the best practice for making a genuine claim.

Whether the claim is against the carrier or the company that loaded the truck, a good photograph is usually undisputed evidence. All carriers have a damage reporting system that can be utilized simply by calling the carrier and requesting a claim form. If there is damaged product on the trailer, it is imperative that the driver of the carrier note "Damaged goods" on the packing slip as evidence of the issue.

LABEL DEFICIENCIES

Very simply, either the supplier label conforms to the company's requirements or it does not. Nissan Motor Company uses complex labels that must specify the part storage location. The system is high maintenance; suppliers must have the capability of tying the releases to the labeling system.

COUNT DISCREPANCIES

The RDR process is a simple way of managing count discrepancies from suppliers. The counting of what has been received can be as simple as verifying the number of containers received to a more labor intensive method of weighing product.

In conclusion, the judgment of how well the receiving system is working regarding data entry can be based on the number of phone calls, letters, and so on that are fielded concerning issues the supplier has with obtaining payment. A visual check of areas where paperwork is being held is necessary. In addition, a visual check of the dock and receiving/inspection areas can indicate how well the process is working. Finally, a weekly generation of the cumulative balances between the supplier and the plant will provide a view of potential issues.

AN ALTERNATIVE SYSTEM

Some companies are now using the receiving data online entry as for the payment process, eliminating the paper invoicing process. The online process requires that the information from packing slips be entered correctly and timely. Since errors made with data entry into the receiving system will result in an over- or underpayment, it is critical that all entries be accurate.

With the online system, a debit or credit of a receipt is simple; however, the system must be capable of generating an adjustment notice to the supplier so that there is a clear audit trail of all transactions. With this system, it is especially important to audit all entries since the supplier is being paid for the material received by the entry.

NOTE

1. The term "MRO" is used to cover any item ordered in the company that is not associated with a bill of materials or capital equipment.

CHAPTER 16

SHIPPING

Depending on how the releases from the customer are generated, the shipping process can be routine or extremely complex. The best practice of knowing what is required to ship is through an electronic data interchange (EDI) process. When the customer sends EDI releases, the supplier has a document that specifies the customer's amount and delivery expectations.

Some customers use a facsimile for the shipment schedule. This method can make it more difficult to track what has been shipped and what is in transit. Facsimiles become outdated shortly after they are sent, and updates for release changes usually are communicated via e-mail or phone calls. The plant is open to errors when an e-mail is not read in time or when someone forgets to convey a change to the shipping schedule.

CUMULATIVE BALANCES

Customers that do not use cumulative balances may create problems for the shipper as well as themselves if they have a poor system of monitoring what is in transit or what has been received. This confusion may result in confrontations between suppliers and customers. Customers may show more products due for delivery while suppliers show an entirely different schedule.

The result of some disputes is expedited freight. Then the issue is compounded by arguing about who must pay the additional freight charges. The best that the shipping plant can do is manually keep track of the shipments and the cumulative balances to the latest release that the customer is sending in order to minimize disputes. If cumulative balances are not used, there is a risk that the plant will not be able to provide proof that product was shipped by the plant on time.

Supplier and customer need to determine how much of an increase in the shipping release within the same week is acceptable. Whenever increases exceed the agreed, the plant should be able to recoup costs incurred over and above the normal process.

ELECTRONIC RELEASES

Customers that use EDI to generate shipping requirements are more likely not to change the release schedule as radically as non-EDI customers are. The reason is that EDI users have better visibility and control over the internal releasing process because they most likely have a full materials requirements planning system that drives their demand.

If the EDI releases are changed up front, the plant materials group can immediately identify the quantity of increase from the previous release by comparing the net change of the two EDI releases. Most computer systems can generate a report that clearly shows the last release detail compared to the most current release detail. The comparison of the previous day's releases to the current day's releases will show the net changes.

A net change report is ideal for challenging premium freight charges or determining if the customer is exceeding the agreed weekly volume.

ANNUAL CUSTOMER VOLUMES

The contracted annual volume expected from the supplier to build and ship is generally a part of all customer contracts. A contract that specifies only the annual volume is open to customer and supplier interpretation regarding weekly build and ship numbers. If there is no provision for maximum weekly ship quantities, the supplying plant may find itself scrambling to make product that was not planned for in the short term and incurring overtime expenses.

All sales contracts must contain a clause that specifies the maximum quantity to be delivered weekly. The contract should state the amount of increase that is acceptable by the supplying plant without penalty during a specified period.

Second-guessing and/or ignoring customer releases can and will spell doom for the supplying plant. Understanding customer release schedules is of utmost importance for managing the plant properly. If the customer requests material over the stated capacity, the plant must respond quickly and identify all of the extra costs.

Letting customers exceed stated capacity without recourse may cause the plant future problems in managing production. Customers should be charged additional labor and machine time for exceeding the stated capacity. It is imperative to address any capacity issue immediately with customers. It is always more difficult to charge customers after the product has been manufactured and shipped.

The best information gathered about customers is not from releases or shipping schedules; it is from proactive direct visits to customers to understand their production process and needs. Understanding customers' production process and materials management functions is invaluable.

Some customers may have a releasing department located separately from the manufacturing plant, perhaps at a corporate office. The major issue with a separate scheduling function is the lack of communication or hands-on planning at the plants. Removed from the real operation, these separate materials departments rely on database information, which may be incorrect and which ultimately may cause havoc for the supplying plant.

OWNERSHIP OF SHIPMENTS TO CUSTOMERS

Customer ownership of the material after it leaves the plant site should never be compromised. Once the material leaves the plant site, the customer should be responsible for handling any carrier issue. If the customer's line is down for lack of delivery, the supplying plant cannot be held accountable.

There are a few rules that a supplying plant should never compromise.

- Under no circumstances should a supplying plant choose an alternate carrier to avoid excess transportation costs. If anything should happen to the freight, the supplying plant is responsible, which may lead to air freight expenses or a worst-case scenario, a line shutdown.
- The supplying plant should never alter the pickup schedule of the carrier or exceed a carrier pick up and leave window of time without the customer's written approval. The best choice is to let the carrier leave as scheduled and then call for another carrier as provided by the customer's procedures.

SHORT SHIPMENTS

It pays to notify customers immediately regarding short shipments in order to obtain a quick status impact on their production requirements. Even if the customer shipments are sent with an advance shipping notification, it is the best practice to call the customer. Understanding the impact of a short shipment to the customer from a supplying plant will result in the least expensive costs from the customer. The customer may decide to waive the remaining balance for the day or add it to the next ship time and day.

SHIPPING ERRORS

One common plant failure is not having the space to stage a shipment. The advantage of staging is the ability to cordon off the area and verify the shipment a second time before it is loaded on the truck. This process does not guarantee perfection, but it does reduce the number of errors.

The most common issues in shipping are the incorrect labeling of product, shipment of the wrong product, and under- or overshipment of product. Even the best scanning systems cannot prevent someone from placing an incorrect container on a truck or placing the wrong label on a container. The best practice to confront these issues is to scan and label the containers at point of entry on the trailer. This process is time consuming and not cost effective, but it can help prevent errors.

Incorrect labeling can be stopped only by comparing the contents of the package to the packing label; however, this method is not 100 percent foolproof either.

The best way to reduce shipping errors is to issue the labels with each shipment, stage the load, apply the labels, and then verify the that the product to be shipped is correct to the pick list.

Under- and overshipments generally are caused by live loading product. Something can go wrong with an unexpected movement of material in a crowded shipping department, causing a shortage or mix-up of containers. As stated earlier, the only effective method of shipping the correct product in a crowded shipping area is to scan the product as it enters the trailer.

CHAPTER 17

CARRIER SELECTION

Getting product shipped and received into the plant on time is crucial to maintaining a smooth manufacturing process. Proper carrier selection is of the utmost importance when the plant requires the product at a specific time and date.

The selection of the correct carrier for the job can be one of the most overlooked areas in a company. Often companies leave the selection of carriers to the plant itself or even to the supplier without regard for the carrier's cost and reliability. If plant shipping expenses are unusually high or if an exorbitant amount of excess freight is incurred, it makes sense to review company policies regarding freight expenses.

ANALYZING FREIGHT EXPENSES

A detailed analysis of the freight expenses incurred for a particular month may reveal the need to implement a freight action plan. An analysis of freight expenses should begin with listing the freight bills by carrier name, type of carrier, the shipment origination, the total freight dollars spent, and the weight of the load. The carrier type should be identified as less-than-truckload (LTL) carrier, full-truckload (FT) carrier, or expedited (E). UPS and Federal Express expenses should also be listed in categories of expedite and nonexpedite. It can be surprising how much money a company can spend using UPS and Federal Express for items that should be shipped LTL.

After all of the freight bills have been listed and categorized, a review by carrier and by carrier-generated bill is necessary in order to understand the expenses incurred.

The simplest method of reviewing the plant's freight expenses to see if there is an immediate opportunity to improve is to examine the freight log by line item and determine if the expense incurred was acceptable or not.

Perhaps the easiest method is to begin with the obvious excessive freight occurrences. For example, LTL carriers charge by weight and impose penalty assessments for using more than the allotted space in the truck. These bills are easy to recognize since the cost of the shipment will stand out when compared to others from the same location.

An FTL carrier should contain at least 40,000 pounds or the truck should have no excess space. Any FTL-designated shipment that arrives with less than 40,000 pounds of material or less than filled to capacity should be considered excess freight.

After the initial review of freight bills is completed, a decision to investigate freight expenses incurred further may be warranted based on the facts uncovered. A second step in the process could be to sort the freight bills by shipping point and then review the costs incurred by the various carriers used to ship the same freight from the same destinations.

Adding a column in a spreadsheet that calculates the cost per pound is an excellent way to compare costs of the different carriers used to deliver the same freight from the same ship point. There could be opportunities to change the amount shipped or the frequency of shipments from a supplier in order to lower the cost per pound.

The process of selecting the correct carrier for the shipment of goods from the suppliers is time consuming but important as it will benefit the company with cost reductions.

FREIGHT MANAGEMENT

In an effort to cut back job positions, many companies have eliminated the corporate traffic manager function. When normal freight costs in the plant are excessive, such a cutback is ultimately a mistake on the part of top management. The concept of pushing the traffic function into the plants does not work well if workers do not have the experience, the desire to manage the carriers, the time to develop the best practices, or the proper direction.

As an option to controlling freight at the corporate level, a few excellent third-party companies can provide a wide range of services for freight management. Companies that specialize in freight management usually offer services such as paying and managing freight bills, managing the carrier base, and providing a hot line for expedited shipments. The cost of having a good freight management service may seem to be exorbitant, but the overall cost savings outweigh the expense.

To manage costs that may be incurred later, it is necessary to understand how to select the best carrier. The foundation for selection must be cost, but the lowest shipment cost is not always the best practice. There must be a careful balance between the cost of a shipment and the carrier's ability to deliver product on time.

In essence, a good carrier is a responsible carrier that will stand by its delivery commitments and will correct mistakes made at no cost to the company. A reputable carrier needs to deliver the product undamaged to the correct location at the correct time.

Proper communications with carriers is also an important part of the success of delivering raw materials on time to the plant. The selected carriers should be able to specify expected arrival times and to know the location of the truck at any given time.

Plants need to develop a reliable carrier base that understands that the amount of business each carrier receives is based on excellence in performance. Excellence should be measured as the number of on-time deliveries a carrier has made to the plant along with the condition of the products delivered.

Working with a few good carriers has a distinct advantage, as carriers pay more attention to companies whose business impacts their bottom line. The relationship between the carrier and the plant is stronger if the carrier manages the bulk of the plant's traffic for a particular territory. Using fewer carriers also saves time involved with managing many carriers that have a small investment in the business. Having fewer carriers generally results in a higher level of concern and customer service, and it enables the plant and the carrier to build a partnership.

Placing the freight bids out for quote with a number of carriers is a good way to evaluate who will be the best fit for the company. A well-defined market in the trucking industry pertains to specific territories and routings that result in the best service at the least cost. These carriers will be identified through the bidding process.

Note that some carriers might have access to areas of the country they service by way of affiliate companies. Carriers that offload freight to affiliates generally create an expense that could be avoided by using a carrier that will handle the freight from point to point.

Pool points are a worthwhile endeavor when numerous shipments come from various points around a central location. Using an LTL carrier to deliver product to a central cross-dock location (generally owned by the LTL carrier) may save the company time and money. It is even possible to load the freight from a pool center of one carrier to a truck from another carrier that specializes in the delivery zone where the receiving company is located.

If possible, use no more than two LTL carriers, with each carrier understanding of the territory they cover and the reasons for the decision.

It is more of a challenge to limit the number of FT carriers, since there may be a wide number of shipping locations spread around the country. Long-haul carriers also have territories where they are most effective and where most of their equipment is based. The best method of developing a solid long-haul carrier base is to determine the traffic lanes that best suit the carrier performance, availability, and the company.

When contracting with carriers, it is necessary to emphasize the importance of on-time delivery and the results of nondeliveries and damaged product. It is advisable to write a carrier contract, but most carriers will refuse this option. The contract should include penalties for nondelivery due to circumstances within the carrier's control, especially if the carrier guarantees delivery.

Carriers need to act with due diligence when faced with an issue that is within their control, such as mechanical failures. Selecting carriers with the ability to replace the cab at the site of a mechanical breakdown has a distinct advantage. No carrier is perfect all of the time, but the carrier that takes prompt corrective action has the edge on others.

Overseas carrier selection should not be difficult; however, it can be a challenge since it is necessary to select a good broker when dealing with overseas shipments. The selection of a broker should begin with locating brokers with operations in the country the company wants to ship from.

When shipments from multiple overseas locations are required, it is best to select a broker that offers global service. The global broker chosen should have operations in most of the necessary ship points.

Many broker services will work with the company to determine the best method of shipping product from multiple locations or to consolidate loads at a common seaport. It is extremely important for a company to request a dedicated container from the broker so that the shipped materials are not likely to be held at customs for paperwork or a container search. A company with a small amount of product to ship may have to ship more material than requested by the customer in order to fill an ocean container which would keep the cost of shipping lower than shipping less material and not filling a whole ocean container with product. The net result of shipping more product is lower freight costs and higher inventory carrying costs; however, it is usually less expensive to carry more inventory than to absorb more freight costs.

There is a variety of different shipping methods for international shipping. It is critical to select the best international commercial terms (incoterms) for the company. A full list of shipping methods and terms can be found by going to the Internet and doing a search on "incoterms."

For most companies, delivery duty unpaid (DDU) or delivery duty paid (DDP) is the best choice. With DDU, the supplier is responsible for getting the parts to the port and shipping the product overseas to the U.S. port selected. The company is then responsible for the customs clearance in the United States and transportation to the plant. With DDU, product liability is in the hands of the seller until it arrives in a U.S. port. With DDP, the title and risk pass to the buyer when the seller delivers goods to the named destination point.

Some other common shipment terms are:

- **Ex works (EXW).** Title and risk pass to buyer, including payment of all transportation and insurance cost from the seller's door. Used for any mode of transportation.
- **Free alongside ship (FAS).** Title and risk pass to buyer, including payment of all transportation and insurance costs, once delivered alongside ship by the seller. Used for sea or inland waterway transportation. The export clearance obligation rests with the seller.
- **Free on board (FOB).** Title and risk pass to buyer, including payment of all transportation and insurance cost, once delivered on board the ship by the seller. Used for sea or inland waterway transportation.

  "FOB" has a different meaning in the United States than in Europe. Internationally, "FOB" is as stated in the internationally widely accepted definition above. There should be no confusion with this term in the United States. "FOB shipping point" in the United States means that the supplier's obligation ends when the product leaves the supplier's dock. In the United States, "FOB destination" means that the seller is responsible for the product until it arrives on the receiving plant's dock.

The selection of a premium land carrier base is as important, if not more important, than the selection of normal transit carriers. The selection of premium carriers depends on the type of service required for the business. Many carriers have onboard tracking systems, which enables a plant to know exactly where the freight is located. Carriers that provide a satellite tracking service charge more for delivery.

Selection of an air carrier is extremely important. Not all premium "guaranteed" freight expediters can live up to their commitments, for various reasons. Freight that has been bumped to a later flight or the next day may cripple the plant; therefore, it is important to understand the premium air carrier's relationship with the airlines so that there are no surprises to the plant.

Although UPS and Federal Express say they can get freight from point A to point B in a day, this is not always the case. In fact, neither of these carriers guarantees any delivery, even with the "guaranteed delivery" packages they advertise. They will use airport delays as a reason for not delivering on time. When these carriers close operations for the day, it is impossible to retrieve essential freight at their location.

At the plant level, in order to keep the inventory levels down, materials control responds to inventory pressures by seeking frequent shipments of components from suppliers. Controlling the inventory level in a plant by using LTL carriers to increase shipments will adversely affect the plant's bottom line by increasing freight expenses. The level of inventory must be carefully balanced against freight expenses. Some analysis is required to make the correct decisions.

Tracking the freight expenses by plant for the entire organization is recommended in order to determine if there are opportunities to combine shipments from common suppliers or common routes for delivery to several plants.

Three graphs and Pareto charts are recommended:

1. Inbound freight expenses
2. Outbound freight expenses
3. Premium inbound and premium outbound expenses

These graphs should be managed at the plant level; there are a number of variables to categorizing the freight expenses that only the plant can manage. For example, the classification of a UPS expense as excess freight may not be correct if the supplier and the plant have recognized that this is the least expensive method of shipment.

One opportunity plants often miss is the charge-back process to the supplier. Some suppliers ship at a premium rate at the customer's expense even when they may be at fault. Plants need to be aware of all premium freight expenses, and it should be the plant's responsibility to debit suppliers when necessary.

Plants generally give their UPS and Federal Express account numbers to suppliers so that shipment charges will be billed to the plant. Some suppliers intentionally or unintentionally use customer account numbers without approval to ship subsequent materials when they are behind schedule. Although it may be difficult to stop this practice, the implementation of the charge-back system for nonapproved premium and excess freight should resolve the issue.

Good tracking involves keeping a logbook to log the premium freight authorizations from the plant. All inbound or outbound shipments must be assigned an authorization number from the plant, if the plant is accepting shipping responsibility. The logbook does not need to be complicated. At a minimum it should specify the date, control number, part number, supplier, mode of transportation, cost (if available), name of the person who approved the freight, and tracking number. The tracking number is important since it enables anyone to determine where a particular shipment is at a given time.

CHAPTER 18

SUPPLIER SELECTION AND RATINGS

Some suppliers are difficult to communicate with, which causes problems for materials personnel. Generally, difficult suppliers usually are those that supply a unique product with little or no competition. In these cases, the plant materials department must ensure that there is a smooth and consistent flow of releases to the supplier. To avoid issues with these suppliers, it may be in the plant's best interests to carry more safety stock in order to avert a production shortage, should the supplier fail to ship on time.

SUPPLIER SELECTION

The basic problem with supplier selection is that a company may focus on obtaining the best price and ignore customer service, on-time delivery, and sometimes quality as prerequisites. The purchasing department is, more often than not, measured on its ability to reduce piece prices and maintain a zero purchase price variance. Purchasing departments have little incentive to deal with companies that are best in all classes, except for price.

Top managers need to weigh the impact of a less-than-perfect supply base with lowest pricing. In the end, the lowest-price supplier may cause issues for the plant, and eventually the plant will absorb the price differences in downtime or quality issues.

Some companies are adopting a supply base rating strategy that is used to award new business. The rating system is generally composed of points awarded by the plant disciplines that are most affected by the supplier base. Materials management awards delivery points, and the quality department awards points for delivery of products to specifications.

Since global competition is moving the main purchasing activity overseas, companies need to exercise extreme care when determining what constitutes the purchasing contact agreement. An air shipment from overseas can quickly reduce or eliminate all of the pricing savings that a company planned to attain by purchasing from foreign competition. Purchasing contracts for overseas procurement should stipulate in detail freight expense responsibility, quality responsibility, and production capacity along with the normal agreement details.

Dispute resolution with foreign-based companies does not always deliver the desired results. Some companies are not cooperative, and there is not much that can be done from thousands of miles away.

In some industries, such as automotive, the selection of the supplier base is narrowing to those suppliers that are the most profitable since the costs of staying in the automotive business is driving those that cannot make a reasonable profit out of business. The impact of the original equipment manufacturer's price reduction demands is taking a toll on suppliers with marginal performance and many of these suppliers are deciding to eliminate their automotive business. The fact that many companies are opting out of procuring and accepting automotive business may eventually lead to a relatively small automotive supply base. When this occurs, suppliers that are left may charge higher costs with out recourse from the major OEMs.

One of the most challenging issues for materials people is managing a supply shortage that has occurred due to scheduling or quality issues. Purchasing contracts rarely contain agreements that stipulate delivery and quality penalties or responsibility. In order to hold the supply base responsible for their actions, contracts need to specify the exact penalties so that suppliers clearly understand what will transpire if they fail to deliver on time.

SUPPLIER DELIVERY RATING SYSTEMS

Ratings from the existing supply base should play an important role in granting additional business to established suppliers. Plants need to do a good job of collecting all of the costs associated with dealing with a bad supplier. Capturing the real costs of doing business with a less-than-adequate supplier will prove invaluable for future contract negotiations.

What constitutes a good supplier rating system? A good supplier rating is based on factual data that can be supported with the appropriate paperwork.

Most manufacturing companies present on-time delivery reports generated by the computer system as the supplier performance document. Computer delivery reports become inaccurate when there is a day or more delay in entering the receiving documentation. An incorrect amount entered into the system can also create a past-due shipment or overshipment.

Some plants recognize that the information in the computer system needs to be screened prior to compiling delivery rating. Often the reports are screened manually by the materials department in an attempt to correct a late delivery that was in fact on time which was shown as late because the packing list from the shipment was entered late. This process is tedious, and most of the time the results are less than desirable.

The supplier delivery rating should also include early shipments. Some suppliers attempt to ship ahead at the end of the month to make sales forecasts. Although it is not good business practice to send early shipments back to suppliers because of the shipping costs that would be incurred, doing so would most likely stop suppliers that consistently break the rules from shipping early again.

In many cases, a computer-generated on-time delivery chart shows poor performance for a supplier that has never expedited freight to the plant or was involved with any downtime issues because of poor data entry timing by the plant.

The reason for showing poor delivery when in actuality delivery was good comes back to timely receipt of paperwork in the system. As an alternative to generating an ineffective computer report of on-time delivery, it is much easier and more effective to create a written document at the time of an occurrence and maintain a supplier file of all late occurrences. It makes more sense to consider a supplier as never late unless the delivery has an impact on production than to try to list the number of late shipments versus the on-time shipments. The concept is simple: If the material is needed and the supplier is late, record the problem; if the material is not needed, consider why the material was ordered. At the end of the month, the nonconformances can be reviewed from the collected documentation.

The main questions to answer with any poor supplier rating is how many expedited shipments did the supplier incur in order to ship product to the plant to avert a shortage or how many occurrences of actual downtime were there due to lack of components? A good practice for tracking on time supplier delivery is to provide the planners with a standardized tracking form that they need to complete for all expedited shipments.

An on-time delivery rating system needs to present realistic information. Any computer-generated information that shows that the majority of the suppliers are not in compliance should be looked at skeptically.

The best system of judging on-time delivery is to measure performance based on the number of supplier-expedited freight shipments, month-end early shipments, and the supplier-caused downtime.

CHAPTER 19

PRODUCTION

Although this book does not discuss establishing production and efficiency rates, the impact that materials control has on operations is discussed here.

A smooth supply of components to keep the manufacturing lines up 100 percent of the time is the goal of all materials management programs. Over the years, many production management concepts have been implemented, revised, and eliminated in an attempt to arrive at the perfect system. Because so much emphasis has been placed on production, materials management has attempted to arrive at the best way to handle conveying production needs to the plant.

PRODUCTION SCHEDULING

The materials department usually is charged with the task of providing the production schedules to the factory floor. There are several methods of conveying production needs to the factory; however, some methods have proven to be more successful than others.

Issuing printed shop orders and the corresponding paperwork should be avoided unless the customer mandates an audit trail with lot control tracking. Government contracts generally call for the tracking of material certifications from all sources of raw materials. A printed work order may be required to track the sources and lot numbers of all raw materials. The completed work order must be maintained on file in the company in case the customer needs to trace raw materials lot numbers to the original sources.

Another form of the production schedule is generated from the personal computer, usually in the form of a spreadsheet. The spreadsheet method of projecting a production schedule is usually inaccurate and untimely. Since no other method in the company may be advanced enough to show the requirements, however, the spreadsheet may be the only option.

ALTERNATIVE APPROACHES FOR PRODUCTION SCHEDULING

The simplest approach for shop-floor scheduling is to allow the shipping system to generate the production needs. This process is managed by the automatic printing of labels that will be used as the authorization to manufacture. To begin the process, the total number of labels for each part number is issued to the manufacturing floor. Manufacturing attaches the labels to the containers, and then the containers are sent to a storage area. When the product is shipped, the computer system generates a replacement label that the materials group takes to manufacturing.

The materials group is responsible for evaluating the number of labels by part number that are in the manufacturing process. The materials group increases or decreases labels based on customer requirements and the plant's safety stock levels. There are two drawbacks to this approach:

1. Possible loss or misplacement of labels
2. Use of production labels for repacking finished goods

The best practice is to compare the number of required labels to the actual label count in the manufacturing cell each day, then add or deduct labels as needed.

The amount of finished goods inventory that needs to be in stock is based on the customer's ship frequency and quantity along with the plant's ability to produce the inventory in the allotted time. Customer shipping frequencies determine the amount of safety stock required to ensure the plant has sufficient time to manufacture the finished goods. For example, a shipping schedule of Monday/Thursday allows for two whole days between Monday and the following Thursday. However, between Thursday and the following Monday there is only one day, unless the plant works weekends.

With the advent of pull systems, many companies are using the concept of red, yellow, and green to identify what finished goods, work-in-progress, and raw materials are required. Each storage area is identified by color, and the finished goods are placed in the area filling the spaces from red through green. This strategy is best suited for plants that have the space to store finished goods at the manufacturing cell. In such cases, managers and operators rely on visual management of stock levels. The materials department needs only to adjust the levels of minimum and maximum amounts for each product.

An alternative to a color-coded storage area is a visual color board filled with production labels. Green is used to indicate that production is on schedule. Yellow can have a number of meanings. It may indicate that the cell needs to produce more product on an overtime basis or at a higher rate to meet shipments. Red signifies that production needs to work overtime in order to meet the customers' shipping schedule.

Another approach is to add an overtime slot to the board to indicate that there is a need to work overtime to complete the day's required production. Any labels remaining at the end of the shift can be moved to an overtime slot to indicate that there was a shortfall. The overtime slot should be marked "bank" or "customer demand." Labels in the bank slots will indicate that the bank level is being depleted. However, there is no immediate impact to customer shipments.

As with any process of managing the finished good inventory, production inventory scheduling depends on the correctness of the actual physical inventory. If the physical inventory is incorrect for any reason, the system will fail. With this in mind, the plant needs to employ a system that has the least potential for errors.

In summary, a visual management system is the best practice for controlling finished good levels. "What you see is what you have" is a system that cannot be challenged as a best practice.

The alternative is to control production requirements by controlling the number of labels issued for the finished product. Labels generated from actual shipments are a way to control production. However, this program can be disrupted when labels are lost, when product is reworked, and when new product labels are issued without conveying the information to the appropriate people.

CHAPTER 20

BEST MATERIALS CONTROL EFFORT

This chapter of best practices is based on the author's years of trial and error and familiarity with many different materials systems. Many companies have adopted some of these systems, but not very many have implemented all of the processes. For this reason, companies continue to face inventory accuracy issues and other related problems.

There is a cost to implementing best practices; however, the cost of *not* implementing these practices may even be greater. It may be difficult to attribute all of the excess costs to poor materials management, but executives need to take a close look at premium freight expenses, downtime numbers, and customer delivery ratings. Except for quality issues driving shortages, no other discipline is more responsible for shortages than materials management.

The best discipline in any organization for mistake proofing and verification systems is in the accounting process of the plant. The accounting process has numerous posting ledgers that all tie into a balance sheet and income statement. Because of the double-checking systems that come with good accounting practices, errors are pinpointed almost immediately. There is no reason that the materials management processes cannot control inventory to the degree that accounting systems provide.

Materials requirement planning (MRP) was developed as a better system for materials management. The inherent issue with all MRP processes is that systems have too many loopholes that allow errors to pass

151

through. For example, in most MRP systems, it is possible to have negative inventory numbers. Negative inventory is an impossibility, but the system processes the information just the same. The materials department must correct the negatives in the system, and many times a shortcut is taken: A simple adjustment is made to the system without fully determining the reason for the negative. Such shortcuts are especially common when the daily negative report is three pages long.

Software programming tied directly into the current MRP system can accomplish most of the best practices in this chapter. As mentioned earlier, there is no foolproof MRP system, but this system is close to perfect.

SAP, one of the world's largest software companies, currently has the software system of choice for many companies because of its ability to integrate all disciplines better than any other MRP system. The problem with SAP is that much of the programming involves the nth degree of accuracy. To prevent some errors that other MRP systems allow, SAP system designers inserted control features that do not allow a transaction to process under certain conditions.

Yet this has created a new problem for SAP users: This system relies on an even higher level of inventory accuracy than previous systems. SAP will freeze transactions from processing when the inventory is not available in the system to support the back-flushing amount.

Another issue with SAP is that the software package is not user friendly. This problem arises in part because SAP is not a U.S.-based package, and the words chosen to describe the inventory action screens are not clear. The verbiage used in SAP is so dissimilar from all other MRP systems in use, such as Oracle, BPCS (business planning and control systems), and QAD (Queen Anne's Drive), that it affects the ability of the materials department to function properly.

BILL OF MATERIALS: A GOAL OF 100 PERCENT ACCURACY

The process of inventory control *must* begin with an accurate bill of materials. There is no excuse for bills of materials to be incorrect.

Bills of materials become inaccurate because no one takes the time to verify them visually at the site of manufacture. There is no process too complicated that cannot be verified on site. If the bills in the MRP system are not 100 percent accurate, the MRP process will be flawed.

If the completed end assembly is small and contains a few components that can be visually verified, it may be a good practice to remove a finished part from the assembly line and take it to an area where it can be checked more easily.

Many companies create bills of materials at the corporate level from part blueprints and drawings. Even if this is the case, a bill of materials is available for the plant to review and correct visually.

PLANNING PARAMETERS: 100 PERCENT ACCURATE

The next step in the best materials control process is correctly entering all of the planning parameters that govern the electronic data interchange (EDI), shipping, receiving, and ordering modules. Every parameter and the outcome of using the parameter in the MRP system must be known in detail prior to their use. A well-defined policy of using planning parameters is mandatory.

The best method for ensuring that the system parameters are correct is to generate reports from the computer system showing the current value set for each part number. If the company does not have reports to verify data integrity, company programmers can create them easily.

BAR CODE SCANNING

The best practice system of inventory control today is using bar code scanning. Bar code scanning offers the most accurate method of inventory control management from on-hand accuracy, to ordering, receiving, and shipping inventory. The basic pitfall is that some bar code systems are incomplete because the system used does not prevent a scan from being missed and the door is left open for errors.

Using bar code scanning to replace manual input only moves the issue from manual errors to missed scanning issues. Much more is required to foolproof the system.

The best scanning process begins with establishing the correct amount of inventory that is required for every component used in the manufacturing process. The criteria for establishing the correct amount of inventory on hand are:

1. Peak production level
2. Ship day(s) from the supplier: Calculated by maximizing freight cost and ship quantity
3. Units per assembly
4. Unit pack size
5. Unit skid size

None of these requirements can be compromised. Each is discussed in detail next.

Peak production is the maximum number of units that the equipment is capable of producing in one day. Arriving at the peak production number may be more complex if the equipment is used for several different finished goods or if the equipment capacity far exceeds customer demand, but it can be accomplished.

In cases where a number of products are produced with the same equipment with no open capacity left over, peak production numbers for each product must be determined by using the highest release amounts for each finished good product in the customer forecast. The result of this analysis will determine if there is enough machine capacity to produce the gross of the peak numbers.

Establishing ship days from suppliers involves considering standard packages, standard skid quantities transit times, and shipping costs. The numbers derived from this data constitute the maximum amount of inventory to be stored in the plant. Units per assembly is the number of components that are used to complete a finished product.

Unit pack size is the number of components that the supplier places in a single package. It is important for supplier and purchaser to agree on the size, weight, and number of components in a container. If possible, unit pack sizes should be ergonomic so that they can be moved easily by hand.

Unit skid size is the number of unit packages that will be stacked together on a skid. Mixed skids of components should be avoided, but sometimes the inventory that would be shipped on a full skid exceeds the plant's short-term need for the component. In this case, the choice is to overstock the components or expend the labor to break down the mixed skid.

CALCULATING THE MINIMUM FOR COMPONENT INVENTORY

The calculation for the minimum balance of components in the inventory is:

$$\text{Minimum inventory} = \text{Round up (Peak production} \times \\ \text{Units required} \times \text{Transit time } (+ \text{Hours/days of Safety stock}))$$

For example, if the peak production is 1,000 finished units per day, the usage for a component part number UMP2000 is 2, the pack size is 250, the transit time is 3 days, then the minimum on-hand balance is 24 unit packs. The 24 unit packs equates to 3 days of raw materials for 3 days of peak production. A safety transit amount needs to be added to protect from late shipments. If peak production is rarely achieved, then a decision to add no transit amount could be an option.

The result for part number UMP2000 is that a maximum of 24 unit packs will be shipped when the minimum balance is obtained. In most cases, less than the 24 unit packs will be shipped since the calculation was based on the peak production number, unless the peak production of 1,000 is produced every day.

DEVELOPING TRANSPORTATION ROUTINGS

After all of the minimum balances are established, the total freight scheduled for less-than-truckload (LTL) shipments needs to be reviewed in order to determine the least costly shipping schedules. The decision to ship raw materials once per week, multiple times per week, or every day needs to be based on total costs. Using space constraints as a determining factor in a decision for shipping components is not cost effective and equates to ignoring inventory as an important part of the manufacturing process. The plant is going to incur costs that could have been avoided if there was floor space assigned in advance for component storage.

After all of the minimum balances and ship quantities are determined, a milk-run schedule or possibly a pool point or cross-dock location for all components that will amount to LTL quantities needs to be developed.

The next step is to develop the routings for full truckload carriers. Pickup days need to be established with the supplier based on the number of shipments required per week. Setting a carrier window time for pickup from a supplier enables the plant to know approximately when it can expect the freight.

If components are purchased from international sources, carrying 40 days of inventory for the minimum is too much and is not recommended. The difficulty with calculating the minimum balance for international shipments is the reliability of the ocean freight to arrive on a weekly basis, which means that some amount of safety stock days must be added. Since ocean freight shipments are unreliable due to weather conditions and other unforeseen issues, there is a high risk of not maintaining a higher inventory than a plant would maintain with land shipments. It is further complicated by requiring the sea container to be full before it is shipped.

When shipping international goods, decisions need to be made based solely on what is right for the company. When sea containers are shared with other companies, the risk is that the other company may not gain timely customs clearance. The best scenario is for the company to have enough of a mix of components that can be shipped at the same time to fill the entire sea container. Whatever the mix, the company has to make the correct decisions to avoid stock-out situations.

It may turn out that the filling of a full sea container will establish the minimum shipping amounts for the raw materials.

In the case of UMP2000, the shipments will come from a supplier that will ship LTL when the minimum balance triggers another release. The 24 standard packages equates to 1 skid of material. Since this is the only raw material this supplier ships, there is also no set day of the week to ship, which gives the plant full flexibility.

CALCULATING THE MAXIMUM INVENTORY LEVELS

Next it is necessary to calculate the maximum inventory levels. This calculation is more complicated since it involves determining the most cost-effective shipping and packaging methods. The lowest inventories using the minimum calculation just described are not always the best practice.

Having the lowest inventories incurs a cost, which is directly attributed to freight expenses and the current cost of cash. Lowering the inventory and raising the freight costs may not be the best practice for the company. The maximum calculation that is presented here is an attempt to balance freight costs and inventory on hand. The twist in the calculation is the cost of cash, which may offset the extra freight costs to keep the inventory lower.

For example, if the cost of borrowing cash for inventory is 9 percent and the cost of carrying fewer inventories for a part is 8 percent more in freight, then the choice is obvious. An excellent practice and a step forward are to use the cost of cash in all inventory-level determinations. Behr America, a supplier of radiators and condensers for the automotive industry, uses the cash percentage in all of its cost of inventory calculations.

The maximum inventory on-hand calculation is the quantity to be shipped by a supplier and received into the plant, plus the minimum balance.

Arriving at the maximum inventory level depends not only on the cost of carrying the inventory; it also depends on space constraints. Space is at a premium in plants, and some plants are not operating efficiently because too much emphasis is placed on cramming as much manufacturing in them as possible. The thought is that manufacturing makes money. This is a true statement, but when the costs of having less-than-adequate systems for materials management are added, it may make sense not to overcrowd a plant with manufacturing.

In a perfect world, the goal is to have the lowest shipping cost per piece with the lowest inventory amount on hand.

For part number UMP2000, the maximum amount on hand will be the minimum of 24 boxes, plus the 24 boxes that are considered to be the economical order quantity from the supplier with the 3-day transit time. UMP2000 will have a maximum of 48 boxes. The assumption is that the cost of shipping is minimal, allowing for a LTL shipment. Part UMP2000 may be a candidate for once-per-week shipping, provided the cost of cash is low and the shipping quantity meets the lowest LTL expense.

DAILY RAW MATERIALS SCANNING IN A CLOSED-LOOP PROCESS

Once the minimum and maximum balances have been established, the scanning system will keep the supplies coming smoothly. The best scanning systems are closed looped. A closed-loop system involves scanning materials from receiving, manufacturing, through shipping.

The best inventory practices involve scanning systems throughout the process. In order to explain the steps in the scanning processes, Scan ABC will be used to illustrate the ordering process.

The ultimate ordering process is to visually scan all of the components by full box content on a daily basis.

How does this ordering process work? All of the components are stored at line side, preferably in gravity-fed racking. New supply is placed in the back, which moves the oldest-dated component containers to the front.

The total number of components is divided among the number of planners, preferably by cell. Every morning, the planners scan all the components that they manage. The scanning equipment contains the information for the minimum and maximum levels. Each planner then enters the number of boxes counted on hand into the scanner. The scanner shows the number of boxes that can be ordered to reach the maximum number. Each planner then decides to order to the maximum, to order less, or to refrain from ordering. These options are an integral part of the ordering process since the planner may know that the assembly process might be down for a few days, which would be an opportunity to minimize the inventory.

In our example, the planner scanned 32 boxes line side and ordered 16 boxes of UMP2000 to obtain the maximum number of 48.

This process eliminates the need for a storeroom for raw materials. The best practice is line-side storage, eliminating all need for warehousing.

If it is not possible for planners to scan all of the components daily, the next best practice is to scan the components from the storage site and then issue the raw materials to the point of use. Scanning begins with the need to move a container from the storage area to the consumption site. The container is scanned, and the scan is recorded into the scanning system as in the previous example, except there is no choice for replenishment. The drawback with this system is issuing a container to manufacturing and failing to complete a replenishment scan.

In both scenarios described above, scanning components as they are moved from the store room or scanning by planners, the scans are sent into a batch file then uploaded into MRP. The process requires planners to scan all of the components they manage and to complete the scanning by a specified time and it allows for all daily scanning to be uploaded at one time. This time must be scheduled and during the morning, after the planners have had a chance to complete the scanning. The alternate scenario of scanning from a storage site allows scans to compile through out the day and allows the uploading of scans into MRP to be more frequent if desired.

MRP is then generated with all of the latest scanning information uploaded. MRP generates planned releases, which are used for determining the labor and capacity requirements.

The ABC scan and other encoded scans generated by the planners becomes a release by MRP, changing the planned releases to firm releases. The ABC scan generated by the movement from stores also becomes a firm supplier release. Part number UMP2000 assigned with scan number ABC now has a firm release for 24 boxes and several months of planned data.

The firm releases are sent to the suppliers in the form of EDI and/or to the company's supplier Web site. Many companies are moving toward using a secure Web site to post the release information for replenishment. This practice is best in class because it allows both the customer and the supplier access to the exact same information, avoiding any communication issues. The supplier Web site may also contain other pertinent information, such as cumulative balance information, leave day, leave time, carrier information, revision level, and so forth.

ABC scan is transmitted to the supplier directly via EDI or to EDI to a commonly shared Web site, taking into consideration the planning parameters for ship day and package size. The supplier will see that the part number is released to be shipped sometime later in the week. In the meantime, before the ship day arrives, the supplier receives other scans for the same part. The gross shipping requirement is the sum of all scans up to the shipping date. Depending on the parameter for shipping the components, the supplier may ship a number of containers, a mixed skid, or a full skid.

SHIPPING AND RECEIVING RAW MATERIALS

The supplier ships the product to the plant and then generates an advance shipping notification (ASN) that informs the plant that the components are in transit. This is an integral step in the ultimate materials management practice, and it should not be overlooked.

Many suppliers do not have the systems to generate ASNs or are unable to receive EDI. Everyone has access to the Web, however. This is one reason why establishing a supplier Web site is so important because it can provide the capability of transmitting ASNs for suppliers.

Once the ASN is received in the plant, the receiving department processes it into MRP as a receipt of material. The ASN information is the receipt, not the scanning of containers received. The next step is to generate plant labels for all of the containers received.

Generating plant container labels from the ASN acts as verification that what the supplier said was shipped is actually what has been received. Each printed label is attached to a container. Any remaining labels indicate that there missing containers from the shipment. A need for more labels means that the supplier shipped more than was transmitted on the ASN.

After the labeling is completed, the supplier is sent a receiving acknowledgment that advises it of any shortage or overage, and the ASN is then corrected.

The ultimate best practice is to invoice the supplier with the ASN information. The payment process is streamlined when payment is made on the ASN amount received into the plant. Since corrections are computerized and immediate, the accounting function becomes easier. If the supplier believes that the plant has made a mistake, it can respond to the ASN correction notice.

SKIP-LOT INSPECTION

The next step is processing the materials that are received through the inspection process. Various quality-control software programs can be used to identify which lots of materials need to be inspected. The skip-lot program interfaces with the system's label generation system. Inspection labels are not printed automatically for containers that must be inspected. These labels are flagged on the system as held for printing. The components on hold for inspection are moved automatically into a location in MRP so that it is clear that the components are on hold.

After quality releases the lot, the quality department sends a release signal to the system and the labels are printed. The inspection label and the ASN printed label are not the same. The inspection label can be as simple as a colored, dated label.

MOVEMENT OF RAW MATERIALS TO LINE-SIDE AREAS

In the best practice, ASN-generated labels also indicate the locations of where the component is to be stored.

The containers are moved to the location specified on the receiving labels. In a storeroom scenario, no specific locations have to be specified. The computer system tracks where all open available places are.

The containers are scanned once they are placed into the storage location to show that there has been a move from the dock location. The latest scanning systems allow lift drivers to remain on the lift while scanning the container into a location.

The process then starts over, closing the loop in the materials management process.

If there is a very large warehouse of components, the best practice is to work with computer-generated pick lists and radio-frequency scanning. This system allows for free flow (using any available space) and guarantees first in, first out since the computer system can be programmed to pick a location that contains the most dated materials. This system maximizes space in the warehouse, since containers can be placed in any available location.

The ultimate system described in this chapter prevents any human data input and output errors from being made in the MRP system. This system is designed to reduce the number of errors that occur in receiving, shipping, storage, and order replenishment.

The ultimate system aids in keeping the inventory accurate but does not resolve all of the issues. The major issue that is left to resolve is scrap reporting, which relies totally on proper reporting.

In the ultimate practice described in this chapter, component replenishment and ensuring there is an unbroken supply of components for manufacturing no longer depends on scrap reporting or inventory accuracy.

Using this process does not mean that the cycle counting should be discontinued. Cycle counting must continue to maintain the perpetual inventory as accurately as possible. The daily scans can be used to compare the inventory on the system to the scanned amounts. Items that have a significant difference should be cycle-counted first.

This process allows metals, for example, to be placed into containers to be scrapped by weight, not by the piece. The net difference between the daily scanned inventory of metal stock (coils and sheet stock) and the perpetual is scrap. The weight comparison of the scrap should equate to the weight of the adjustments made to the perpetual inventory by component part number.

In Exhibit 20.1 is a closed loop materials management process that will provide the best practice for success.

If this system of inventory sounds easy, it is.

EXHIBIT **20.1** *Ultimate Materials Process*

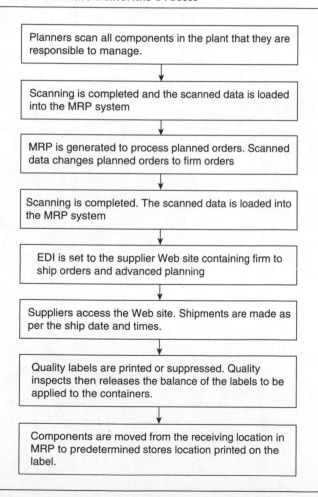

CHAPTER 21

ADVANCE LOGISTICS PLANNING

What is advance logistics planning? In short, it is the process of calculating the costs of transportation and packaging for quotes (acquisition) to the customer base and/or the continuous planning before the customer order is ready for production (series production).

Many companies do not employ advance logistics planning. Those that do find that they are able to price what they sell better. Understanding transportation costs and packaging costs will enable purchasing and management to make better decisions that are truly cost based.

Advance planning takes place at the quoting stage with the customer. An understanding of the transportation costs and the packaging costs, even if estimated, is better than adding a standard percentage to the quote. Quoting with estimated logistics costs is especially important when there is a question about where raw materials, subassemblies, and finished product are to be sourced.

The company may choose to source to a supplier that is the farthest distance from the plant, even though comparable suppliers are closer. In order for a company to make the best supplier selection, all of the costs associated with procurement must be considered. This means that the cost of international transportation, including all fees associated, must be included in the piece price when comparing the costs of components made and shipped within the United States with those made internationally.

Companies with global holdings may purchase components from overseas sister companies without much regard to the transportation and packaging costs. The risk here is that air-freight costs may erase all intended savings. When making a decision to purchase overseas or in the United States between plants in the same family, the lowest labor rates are usually the deciding factor. However, raw materials costs may sway a decision to make in the United States or source overseas within a family of plants.

The formula for the make-or-buy decision is:

$$(\text{Raw material cost} + \text{Overhead costs} + \text{Transportation costs} + \text{Packaging costs})/\text{Number of pieces shipped}$$

The decision may be different if the overseas company is not a part of the U.S. family of companies. If the U.S. company can make the product and open capacity is available, making the part may be in the best interests of the U.S. company, even though the final price of the part is less expensive overseas. Leaving capacity open or idle does not make good business sense, especially when the risks of overseas procurement are much higher.

It is difficult to put a price on the cost of quality when components received from overseas do not meet specifications or there is a high potential for premium freight. These potential costs are rarely considered in management decisions because everyone is convinced that no extra costs will be incurred and product price takes precedence.

The plant suffers with high costs when something goes awry with a supply delivery from an international source with expensive air freight costs. The excess freight costs incurred are almost never associated back to the price of an overseas part versus buying the part made in the United States. If the real costs incurred over a period were added to the piece price of the component, overseas sourcing might be questioned. It makes sense to review overseas sourcing at least once per year and determine if doing business with that supplier truly saves the company money.

Component size and complexity should be considered when deciding where to source. A calculation of the cost to air-freight components from the overseas source to the United States should be a part of the calculation of doing business.

The larger and more complicated the part is, the more it will cost to air-freight the part to the United States. In many cases, the air freight actually incurred is for an air-charter, which usually negates the anticipated piece price savings of the international sourcing over a long period of time. At least one air-charter cost needs to be calculated and added to the piece price of the part that is slated to be purchased internationally in order to understand the impact on the potential cost savings of doing business internationally. The decision-making calculation then becomes:

Raw material cost + Overhead costs + Packaging costs +
1 air charter cost / Number of pieces required for 12 months

For example, the raw material and overhead are $10.97 per part. An air charter cost is calculated at $9,000. The number of parts that can be shipped for the $9,000 is 100. One hundred parts will cost $90 each to ship via air freight. Considering that 30,000 parts are required for a year, air-shipping the parts will add an estimated $.30 to the cost of each part. In the example, the quoting cost would be $10.97, plus $.30 for a total of $11.27. With this new calculation, will an overseas purchase still be competitive?

Some executives may consider this calculation radical. The best way to prove whether it is or not is to ask the question: How much money has the company spent on air freight from overseas suppliers? The answer may be surprising; it is likely to be very high for a number of reasons.

Materials people often run into supply issues when the overseas supplier fails to make product on a timely basis or the method of controlling inventory leaves much to be desired. Based on this author's experience as a director of several large automotive concerns, I can safely say that there has never been a plant that has not been involved with air-chartering parts from an overseas supplier. This fact is generally related to the lack of cycle-counting key components or the rampant generation of useless release data from a materials requirement planning (MRP) system. As explained in earlier chapters, corrupt input and output information is the root cause of poor releases and inventory inaccuracies.

The cost of quality is more difficult to determine, and the decision here may be purely subjective. A sound subjective decision about quality ensures that the likelihood of a serious quality issue is low and therefore the risk of procurement from overseas is low. Attaching a dollar figure to the cost of quality is difficult but not impossible. Using the previous calculation for air-chartering parts may offer the answer. Keep in mind that additional expenses may need to be added if a quality person has to fly to the supplier.

Advance planning should encompass the complete process of tracking and managing all components in a program launch from the start to the end. Advance planning is complete when the job is in full production and the responsibility transfers to plant logistics. The plant planning group should take the control of planning from a production-ready status otherwise, the logistics task must remain with the advance planning group.

Advance planning involves a team of people led by a program manager who is responsible for the entire launch. The program manager is the person who negotiates the contract with the customer and then ensures that every detail is followed in the pre-production timeline up to and including the full production status.

The team usually consists of members from every discipline involved in procurement all the way to getting the finished goods production ready. Team members may include purchasing, planning, process engineering, supplier quality, customer quality, industrial engineering, transportation, advance planning, and packaging.

The program manager who leads the team is responsible for maintaining a detailed timeline and action list. The action list is updated on a weekly basis. Any discipline that falls behind in its assigned actions is reviewed by the next reporting level in the company.

The program manager is responsible for reporting to senior staff. At the senior staff meeting, the manager discusses the timeline along with any critical or red action items.[1] Senior staff then needs to address any red items by calling on the department managers or directors for resolution. The president of the company needs to be informed about any issue that will directly affect meeting customer due dates.

In the advance planning realm, control and follow-up are critical. Every part number from the bill of materials must be detailed out. The detail that advance planning follows is crucial to having the correct components at the correct time. The advance planning matrix may look like the example in Exhibit 21.1.

The matrix contains many categories. A great amount of work needs to be completed just in the materials area to launch a product. Problems with any of the categories shown in the exhibit could result in a failure to obtain materials in the correct quantity at the correct time.

Detailed Explanation of Each Category

Line Item: List each component by line item, 1, 2, 3, etc.

Part Level: Latest release number for a part, for example, revision A, B, etc.

Purchased Part (PP) or manufactured (M)

Carry-Over Part: Is the part used in another process?

MRP Setup: Is the part set up in the system with the correct planning parameters?

PPAP'd (production part approval process): Is the component approved to be manufactured by the supplier?

Packaging Approved: Has the packaging been approved for the supplier to use for component shipments?

Packaging Purchased: Has the packaging been purchased to ship components from the supplier to the plant?

EXHIBIT **21.1** *Typical Advanced Logistics Worksheet*

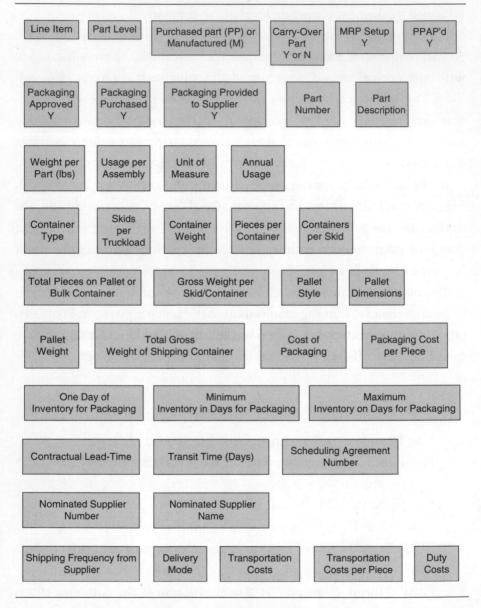

Packaging Provided to Supplier: Does the supplier have the packaging on site to use for shipments?

Part Number: Enter the component part number of the supplier sourced component.

Part Description: Enter the description of the supplier sourced component.

Weight per Part (lbs): Enter the part weight—this is critical for calculating ergonomic containers for the assembly-line process.

Usage per Assembly: Required for purchasing the correct quantity for manufacturing.

Unit of Measure: pieces, kilograms, pounds, etc.

Annual Usage: Important in calculating freight costs and stock levels.

Container Type: Enter the type of the container. Is it corrugated or returnable?

Skids per Truckload: Important in calculating freight costs and deciding full-truckload or less-than-truckload shipments.

Container Weight: Enter the weight of one container.

Pieces per Container: Used for supplier release planning, freight, floor space calculations.

Containers per Skid: Used for calculating floor and rack space, minimum quantity on-hand calculations, and freight calculations.

Total Pieces on Pallet or in Bulk Container: Calculated from pieces per container times the number of containers on a skid, or enter the number of pieces to be shipped in a bulk container.

Gross Weight per Skid/Container: Used to calculate the total weight of the shipment.

Pallet Style: Enter plastic, wood, or corrugated.

Packaging Information

Pallet Dimensions: Enter the length, width, and height of the pallet.

Pallet Weight: Enter the weight of the pallet (for freight calculations).

Total Gross Weight of Shipping Container: Used for freight calculations.

Cost of Packaging: Enter the cost of packaging.

Packaging Cost per Piece: Calculated from the cost of packaging divided by the number of pieces per container.

One Day of Inventory Packaging: Based on the expected sales number of units per day equated to number of packages required.

Minimum Inventory in Days for Packaging: Number of packaging units required for a set number of days production.

Maximum Inventory in Days for Packaging: Number of packaging units that are required to fill the supply chain.

Logistics Information

Contractual Lead-Time: Enter the lead time for the supplier to make product from their raw material procurement time, plus manufacturing time, plus shipment ready time. Used for procuring component supply beyond the agreed amount to be manufactured and shipped in a period of time.

Transit Time (Days): Delivery from ship date to plant into date.

Scheduling Agreement Number: Enter the supplier/plant purchase order number.

Nominated Supplier Number: Enter the company-assigned supplier number.

Nominated Supplier Name: Name, address, telephone number, contact name, etc., in additional fields.

Shipping Frequency from Supplier: Enter the number of times the components are shipped from the supplier or enter the day(s) of the week parts are shipped.

Delivery Mode: Enter the mode of shipment (LTL, FT, ocean freight, etc.).

Transportation Costs: Enter the total cost of a shipment from the supplier to the plant.

Transportation Costs per Piece: Divide the total transportation costs, including any duties or associated fees by the total number of pieces in the shipment.

Duty Costs: List the total costs associated with any international shipment pertaining to duty and taxes.

Depending on the nature of the business, additional categories may be required. For example, some companies maintain dual sourcing.

The administration of advanced logistics planning is instrumental in the success of the launch. Perhaps this complexity is why companies fail when they try to manage logistics from the plant planning or from individual functions.

The computation of packaging, shipment, and piece price cost are not the complete function of advance logistics since much of this information must be placed into a timeline that needs to be managed at least weekly. Advance logistics must also hold separate meetings and maintain a separate action item listing from that of the program manager.

As a part of superior project planning, purchasing should have a number of disciplines involved with any sourcing decision which may include quality, engineering, and materials control. A matrix rating all potential suppliers needs to be created so that suppliers are selected not just on price alone but include a quality rating, an engineering rating, and a delivery performance rating. Some form of calculating the final rating of each supplier needs to be developed. This topic, which depends on the nature of the business, is beyond the scope of this book.

A supplier that is awarded business should be called into a meeting with the various disciplines to verify the procurement process. For example, the advance planner needs to know whether the supplier has read the packaging and logistics package and that the supplier agrees to the conditions outlaid in the manual. Some questions to ask: Is the supplier capable of transmitting advance shipping notifications? Is the EDI tested and ready? Is the packaging complete? Does the supplier have packaging and a backup plan? Is the part to be supplied approved and ready to be supplied in the proper container? Does the supplier have routing information to ship the parts to the plant? Who is the primary contact from the supplying plant? Who is the emergency off-shift contact in the supplying plant? Who in the supplying plant is capable of setting up emergency shipments in a timely manner?

The advance planner always must be aware of the bill of materials timing, which is the most critical part of the planning process, since without it advance planning cannot occur. Sometimes not having a complete bill of materials is a roadblock to advance planning since engineering may have difficulties meeting the timeline due to customer changes. Engineering should and must provide a partial bill of materials. Some companies call this an A or B release, and the bill of materials is not completed and released for production. An A release may be a concept bill of materials with no part numbers assigned. The A release may be a copy of several existing bills that are similar and serve to provide quoted costs. The B release may be a partial release based on those parts of a subassembly that are ready for production. The C release may be the completed bill of materials that can be used to order components.

Advance planning, engineering, and purchasing must work together closely when the bill of materials is at the B release level, because many components will need to be purchased on spot buys. Spot buys are component purchases that are made before the supplier contract is signed or before the final tools are available in order to obtain materials for pre-production needs. Some companies leave the spot buying to the engineering or purchasing departments since the parts involved usually are used in the prototype shop, and they are made from soft tooling. These parts must always be carefully marked so that they do not end up on the production-ready shelf.

The advance planner must work closely with the plant's industrial engineer to develop the plan to store components in a warehouse or line side. The planning of the line-side storage quantities is the direct responsibility of the advance planner, although the finalization of the plan rests with plant planning management.

The advance planner needs to be in constant contact with plant planners so that they are kept in the loop. The advance planner must stay with the program until sufficient quantities of all production-ready components are in the manufacturing plant. Once all issues concerning production-ready components are resolved, the advance planning function has ended. Plant planning takes over the task of obtaining and maintaining production-ready component deliveries.

The advance planning activities can be broken down into four segments.

1. **Acquisition.** Advance logistics is involved with quoting the piece price costs for sales and marketing to use in negotiating with potential customers.
2. **Design.** Planning activities are minimal in this stage and usually are restricted to a few quotes. This is the phase where engineering actually designs a prototype part for the customer.
3. **Preseries.** Preseries is a word commonly used to identify all of the activities in a company that take place before the product is actually produced for production. This is where most of the logistics activities occur.
4. **Series.** Series planning is where the actual production-ready parts are produced and shipped to the customer. This segment marks the end of advance planning and start of plant planning.

NOTE

1. Many companies use color coding to code action items from least critical to critical. Green usually denotes on-time progress, yellow indicates that some parts of the action item are lagging behind the target date, and red indicates critical progress or past the target completion date.

MEXICAN PLANTS

The best practice for managing Mexican operations is to begin with an understanding of the culture. The cultural difference in Mexican plants poses a particular problem for those who are sent on missions to train and educate. A good start to understanding the Mexican culture is to obtain a modern-day cultural book that has been authored by a Mexican National who is a leading expert on Mexican culture. A genuine understanding of the cultural differences between the United States and Mexico goes a long way in making plants run more smoothly.

The cultural differences are not the only problem managers face; another problem is the ability of the English speakers to convey what they want the people to understand and learn. People sent from the United States to train personnel in Mexico need to speak slowly and clearly. They also need to choose words that are commonly used. Many Spanish words are similar to English words; the use of these words will help people to get their point across easier. Speaking Spanish is not a necessity. Without at least a basic knowledge of the proper pronunciation, attempting to speak the language does more harm than good. Tapes and other resources to learn the proper pronunciation is a start.

The Mexican people in the office enjoy conversing and getting to know people. Being personable goes a long way in gaining their trust and understanding. Demanding and autocratic people generally will not be accepted.

If you are invited to a function, it is to your advantage to attend. The functions are generally birthday parties, retirement parties, and other events that Mexicans enjoy as a family. A friend you make in Mexico is a friend forever, no matter how distant the relationship becomes.

In any cultural situation, it is important to ensure that what is said in words is what is interpreted. It is best to ask the person to reiterate what they think you have said as instructions. It is not good to use vocabulary that is not understood. It is best to stick to common words.

When people of different languages speak to each other, it should be at a pace that everyone can understand. Not everyone will understand and interpret rapid English in the same way. Many Mexicans understand English very well; others may not. You are likely to get a yes answer just to satisfy you so it is important to use care when speaking.

Since many people do not speak English, learn how to ask for directions in Spanish. Americans find it easy to get lost in Mexico because there are not many signs with route numbers. Knowing the street names will be beneficial when traveling to and from the hotel.

Practices and methods taught to the lowest levels of the organization may never be implemented if the hierarchy does not understand the benefits of the action plan. Mexican leadership is based on a hierarchy that is unbroken from the bottom up. Rarely does one level bypass the next.

People generally carry out any instruction from a higher level without question, even if it goes against their training and the known correct process.

It is not only the good training and the implementation of sound practices that leads to success; it is also the selection of leaders. However, locating leaders with the knowledge required to operate the systems successfully may not be an easy task in the future. The explosion of new businesses may strain the availability of knowledgeable people in the field.

It may be beneficial to mentor in the United States people who will eventually return to Mexico. This gives the person time to adjust to the company and to the people in the other plants or in the corporate office. In addition, it gives the person an opportunity to learn more about the American culture and the language.

Providing the proper training and coaching is not an easy endeavor for some U.S.-based companies since Mexico is not regarded as the safest place to visit. Training through seminars and meetings in the United States may fail since there is no guarantee that the intended practices will be retained, accepted, or even implemented.

American companies waste thousands of dollars with consulting and instruction and not enough time with hands-on training. Hands-on training is the best method to set in place materials control practices that will benefit the company in Mexico. Evidence for this comes from my own experience with developing a materials team that became highly proficient in managing and reducing inventory from $25 million to under $7 million in one short year even while doubling the plant's sales. To accomplish this, management was willing to spend countless days and nights in Mexico to provide a foundation for future plant management. Today, the plant is the most successful and profitable division in its group.

In summary, the best practice to implementing a solid materials system is to provide the necessary in-plant training and follow up to ensure that the methods and practices have the correct outcome. Understanding the culture of Mexico or any country in which a plant is located is the best practice.

MANAGEMENT PHILOSOPHIES

Over the course of my years in management for major automotive tier two suppliers, I have noted some of my better management decisions. I have learned by trial and error over my 30-year career to develop a management style that works the best with the people I led.

Early in my career as a manager, I made many mistakes in supervising people that today I would consider bad management practices. Management is a trial-and-error process. You need to always look back to see where you could have improved and take the best practices to the next level.

What led to my best practices of management were the deplorable management practices by some of my superiors. In the late 1980s to this day, some executive managers began considering people not as assets but as replaceable parts. I have heard executives tell people that they are lucky to have a job and are privileged to work for the company. This type of thinking generally leads to an arrogant approach toward people, which does nothing to motivate employees. Some executives believe that they do not need to motivate employees because everyone is replaceable at any time.

Executives and those who manage for them no longer can achieve any longevity in companies because of that management thought process. In the early 1970s, people could expect to work for a company for as long as they wanted, as long as they accomplished the goals and objectives that were set forth. Today, even managers who meet goals and objectives and obtain good reviews and raises may find themselves without a job when upper management changes, which it does frequently.

In the automotive sector, strong competition means that some executives and managers are driven from the company within two years. The company's need to make profits that satisfy the stock prices has taken precedence over any moral values. Companies that were once considered people companies have lost their identity and begun adopting a view that people are the problem.

The frequent chief executive officer (CEO) changes in automotive supplying companies have led to a complete loss of company identity. With every new CEO comes a host of philosophy and general operations changes. Each new CEO promises to increase stock value by improving the company's cash flow and profits.

The problem is that earlier CEOs have cut capital expenditures to the point that the equipment no longer generates the returns that it was once capable of producing; therefore promises of increasing efficiency or cash flow is thwarted. In addition, most of the established talent pool has been replaced with less expensive managers. As an example, a plant that I worked for until 1998 is posting a salary for the same position for less money in 2008. This means that, in 10 years, the salary for this position has actually decreased.

Because of the high CEO turnover, all later CEOs inherit plants where the resources have reached a point of no return. I have been in automotive tier two and three plants where the capital investment for the year is near zero and the aging equipment is beyond its intended life expectancy. The equipment repair costs have escalated in some plants beyond reason because of the lack of investment.

CEOs are forced into short-term thinking because their predecessors used up all operating capital. Many times the first thought of a CEO is to replace people because the plant is missing a profit goal; however, the goal may always have been virtually impossible. Most intelligent managers will recognize that the equipment was so decrepit that they could not make the bottom line and thus lost their jobs. Many business sectors are in an endless game of hire and fire that leads nowhere and accomplishes nothing.

Despite all this, the philosophies in some companies honestly work to augment management practices. Nothing stops executives from maintaining a good management style even when they have inherited a seemingly impossible position. We have to realize it is not necessarily the people who do not make it happen; it is the circumstance we place them in.

I have created a list of philosophies that have worked the best for me over the years. In some cases, it took many years of trial and error to make the correct decisions and adopt the philosophies that work the best in all situations.

When I was younger, I considered myself a bad manager. I was definitely confused as to how a good manger should operate. To become a good manager, one must be looked on as a good leader. The only way to become a good leader is to earn the support of the people you manage.

Here's a list of philosophies that have worked best for me over the years.

- If someone chronically complains about another group, transfer that person to that group. The understanding they gain from being in that group is invaluable.
- In a crisis, work at the level of the group in trouble to help them recover. (Borrowed from Lee Iacocca.)
- Manage by showing people the best practices and letting them implement the actions and make minor changes.
- Lead by actions and others will follow.
- Make people laugh in a crisis mode. Make the recovery plan fun.
- When people need to work long hours on a project, make sure they all leave early on a Friday night. The respect you gain is invaluable.
- Give people three chances to make it happen, the fourth time do it yourself, and make the fifth time the last time.
- In a bad situation, make sure people understand how serious you are! Use force as a last resort. (Borrowed from Abraham Lincoln.)
- Use clear communication, be concise, and stay the course.
- A good leader avoids issuing orders, preferring to make suggestions, imply, or request. (Borrowed from Abraham Lincoln.)
- Never let anyone abuse your authority or disrespect you. (Borrowed from Ronald Reagan.)
- Seek the consent of your followers to lead them.
- Never crush people, making them and their organization enemies. (Borrowed from Abraham Lincoln.)
- Always lead by example, get results and more results.
- Never fill a plant with people who know each other. It will eventually cause you grief.
- Take out those who are not serious or those who undermine progress.
- Take charge of a bad situation, be undoubting, and stay the course.
- Do not ask permission from your superiors. Let them tell you when to stop.
- Seek the help of those who can add value to your cause.
- When in a crisis, work at the lowest levels.
- Do not let your peers bash your efforts. Make sure they understand your position.

- Do not accept poison pen letters. Note your dissatisfaction; it scares them off.
- You catch more flies with honey than vinegar.
- If you mediate, ensure both sides have a clear understanding of what the facts are.
- State nothing but the facts to your superiors and be able to support them with evidence.
- If you make a mistake, admit it and move on.
- Do not dwell on the bad; look for the good.
- If at first you do not succeed, try again, then take them out.
- Touch people with your best. (Borrowed from Abraham Lincoln.)
- Stand up to unjust criticism. (Borrowed from Abraham Lincoln.)
- Look at both sides of a story.
- Those who complain the most usually have the dirtiest house.
- Always, always end a decision-making conversation with "Do you agree?"
- Do not let anyone misconstrue a situation.
- Listen; you might learn something.
- Take no prisoners when you are out of time.
- Clean house when the deck is stacked against you.
- Make sure your subordinates understand why their idea is not the best for the company at this time.
- Exercise a strong hand and be decisive. (Borrowed from Abraham Lincoln.)
- Surround yourself with winners. Ask the losers to get on board or lose them.
- If your superior needs to approve every move, find another job.
- Do not let your superiors interpret a situation incorrectly from another source. Speak up or forever hold your peace.
- Do not let someone use words that place you on the defensive for a bad situation. Let them know your dissatisfaction with the way in which they describe the situation.
- Make your vision clear to all. Be result oriented.
- When someone points the finger, break it off with the facts.
- Catch a rat with the best mousetrap.
- Never let anyone put you on the spot. (Borrowed from Ronald Reagan.)
- Sometimes people are putting out small fires when they have a whole forest burning behind them. Make them stop and look at the big picture.

- Extinguish the fire by pushing people to do the correct things.
- Promote those who promote you.
- Always let people know when they are doing a good job.
- Those who spend all of their time making others look bad are bad.
- Never lose the respect of those you lead; it will kill you. (Borrowed from Abraham Lincoln.)
- If you play both sides of the fence, it will eventually fall on you.
- When you cut heads, make sure you cut the right ones.
- In a losing situation, sometimes you have to invest more.

COLOR CODE MANAGEMENT STYLES

Over the years, I have come across many types of management styles and personalities. Over the years, I have come to realize that everyone fits into a few basic categories at varying degrees. Recognizing these personalities can help you make decisions when dealing with people. Engineers, for example, are not quick decision makers in general, nor should they ever be quick decision makers.

I began to color code management styles around 1989 when faced with a host of management styles from the staff I worked with. This was the most diverse staff in terms of management styles that I had—and have—ever encountered. The variety of personalities enabled the plant to increase sales from $7 million to over $150 million in two years. Without the diversity in personalities, there may not have been any stability in the organization. As it turns out, the entire staff was replaced or left to pursue other opportunities when new top management took over. Since that time, the plant has not been able to achieve the levels it once accomplished.

Below is the color-coding of personalities that I have come up with. The colors I have selected have no relationship to any other organization that may use color coding. The selection of colors is meaningless, and I could have chosen any color. The descriptions are the important part of the discussion.

- **Red.** Red managers make quick and decisive decisions. They sometimes shoot first and ask questions later. These managers do not always consult with others for agreement, especially if the managers are already convinced of the outcome. They formulate strong opinions and rarely budge

from them. These managers get things done immediately, even if the outcome is not always the best.

- **Yellow.** Yellow managers are excellent communicators and good listen-
  ers. Their actions and decisions are based on consulting others and on
  group consensus. They carefully concentrate on understanding the impact to others before making final decisions.
- **Blue.** Blue managers' plans are well thought out by weighing the impact
  of all alternatives. These managers listen to others but may keep the
  course. They make decisions carefully based on the best facts available.
  Blue managers pay attention to details and gather information to ensure
  that the best outcome is achieved.
- **Purple.** Purple managers spend an excessive amount of time weighing all
  the alternatives and then reevaluate the circumstance to ensure correctness. These managers may not make the final decision until a complete
  consensus is reached or they are forced to make a final decision. To these
  managers, timelines are not as important as getting the decision made
  correctly.

Some managers may think that they operate in any one of the categories I
have described based upon the particular circumstance. The truth is that there
are times when you really do need to operate in a different management mode.
Personalities are complex, but regarding your position in the company, most of
the time you are likely to operate in one of the zones I have described.

Some personalities fit better in some jobs than others. An accountant would
never be able to get the books correct without detailed analysis capabilities. An
accountant who made only snap decisions without weighing all of the consequences would not survive on the job. A good accountant must operate in the
blue mode.

Materials people perform best when they have more of a blue-type personality. Materials people need to evaluate and weigh the impact of all of the alternatives before making a final decision. They have to be detail oriented,
especially when interpreting inventory needs and how to manage a crisis with
the least impact to costs. A purple-type person might be able to function in a
level where quick decisions are not required.

A human resources (HR) person is more apt to be a yellow-type person. HR
people must be able to deal with the many personalities of people that they
encounter. They must have the ability to listen well and communicate at all
levels. An HR person at the red level is not likely to achieve success interacting

with people. In my career, I have met some red HR managers. The red manager is not well liked and, most likely, you will not find very many people in the manager's office.

A chief executive officer (CEO) may be more of a red-type person. A CEO needs to make firm decisions in order to move the company forward, get things accomplished, and drive staff in the right direction. Most CEOs have their own ideas about how to manage successful operations, and they rarely change their methods of management. It would not hurt for a CEO to have a yellow-type personality, especially in a service-type industry.

Engineers tend to be more of the purple type. Many engineers will take an excessive amount of time to make a decision. This trait is good to have when you are building something that needs to be perfect. When engineers are planning to build a bridge, a dam, or a high-rise building, they need to take their time to ensure everything is exact in mathematical terms and quality of materials used. If an engineer made a snap decision on a bridge specification, we might all be in trouble. Many of the best products on the market are well thought out by engineers who take the time to assess and reassess the product.

A good quality person should have similar personality traits as a materials person. Both need to gather all of the data required to make the correct decisions. A quality person has to pay attention to details and has to have the capability to understand if something is in the specification or outside of it.

Good plant managers should be able to make quick and decisive decisions based on staff input. The best staff consists of people who fit into the color modes that best suit the type of job. Plant managers should welcome engineers who are looking to make the best product possible and not ones who are going to make quick decisions that result in issues for the plant down the road.

There are and should be varying degrees of colors in a personality when it pertains to managing people in the work environment. A manager could be considered a red and blue manager. In this case, the manager makes decisions that are in the red mode when necessary but works in the blue mode most of the time.

The idea is to get the executive manager into thinking about the personalities in the company and how best to smooth out the organization using all of the different management styles.

Managers may fail when they are forced to operate in modes that they are not used to or feel comfortable. Pushing a manager to make quick decisions when he or she is used to evaluating the options usually spells disaster for the company and the person. It is best for the company to ensure that people are able to work comfortably in the job that they were hired to accomplish without forcing a change in management style.

Companies should strive to have a number of different management types in the organization. An organization filled with quick decision makers might produce products that do not satisfy the needs of the customer base. It would be tragic if a product were recalled that was based on a quick decision instead of a process that included analysis and testing.

INDEX